Texas

A Captivating Guide to the History of Texas and Texas Rangers

Free Bonus from Captivating History
(Available for a Limited time)

Hi History Lovers!

Now you have a chance to join our exclusive history list so you can get your first history ebook for free as well as discounts and a potential to get more history books for free! Simply visit the link below to join.

Captivatinghistory.com/ebook

Also, make sure to follow us on Facebook, Twitter and Youtube by searching for Captivating History.

Contents

Part 1: History of Texas

A Captivating Guide to Texas History, Starting from the Arrival of the Spanish Conquistadors in North America through the Texas Revolution to the Present

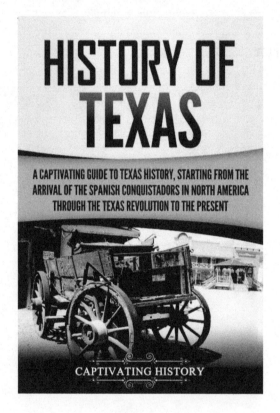

Introduction

Texas is one of the most recognizable states in the United States of America (it is the second-largest, behind Alaska), and it also has a reputation for being unlike any other. This reputation is well-deserved, in part because of the state's long and often contentious history. That history has fascinated many people not only in this nation but around the world for centuries. From the heyday of the Wild West and the state's oil boom to the storied Texas Rangers and the construction of one of NASA's primary facilities, it seems nearly impossible to fully explore everything in the state's rich past.

While the real history isn't nearly as well-known as the stereotypical images of Texas, the state has a past that dates back millennia before the arrival of Europeans in North America. The native peoples had a diverse range of cultures and beliefs – much more diverse than the few religions practiced in Europe. These original inhabitants adapted to the different environments in the vast areas of the state, carving out existences with knowledge and rituals that have largely been lost to time and the arrival of the Europeans. Even the name "Texas" derives from a Native American term that was adopted by the Spanish as they started to persecute and displace the native peoples.

The Spanish and French were the first Europeans to explore the expansive lands. Their arrival initiated the first major shift in the genetic makeup of the region's population, setting the stage for several centuries of struggle as newcomers sought to take control of the native people's lands. Texas was always a highly desirable region due to its many natural resources and limitless potential. For several centuries, it served as a fertile place for cattle ranches, cotton farms, oil fields, and as a source of timber.

Both the Spanish and the Mexicans recognized how valuable the territory could be, but neither country had enough people to settle the region. The solution seemed obvious: they invited Americans to move into the territory and settle it. Of course, this invitation came with several stipulations, including one that required the Americans to give up their citizenship and trade primarily with Mexico. The chief problem was that the invitation to settle the region was extended while Mexico was fighting Spain for their independence. This decade-long war would affect the relationship between the settlers and the newly-forming country of Mexico.

There would be many contentious points between the American settlers and Mexico, two of the biggest being slavery and the unstoppable flow of new settlers rushing into the territory. The settlers had also largely been responsible for their own protection against Native Americans and bandits who prowled the countryside, which left the homesteaders with no sense of connection or mutual interest with their host nation. Over time, yearning for total autonomy ended in revolt, and the territory of Texas became independent. For nearly a decade, Texas was its own nation. However, many of the people living there had American roots and were struggling to get their new country admitted into the US—a risky move that would almost certainly result in war between the US and Mexico.

When the US finally agreed to annex Texas, American politicians had already formed a plan to ensure the acquisition of even more land from Mexico. Mexico was a new nation, while the US had been an independent nation for more than half a century and had built a robust military. However, the annexation of Texas ultimately became one of the causes of the American Civil War. Though it was still a new state, Texas seceded with the rest of the slaveholding states. This proved to be the one war that the intrepid Texans would not win. Texas recovered relatively quickly, however, from the devastation of so much fighting, largely due to the many highly desirable resources available in its vast territory.

Texas is also home to some of the nation's most infamous criminals and has some of the most notorious settings from the Wild West era. For many years, Texas seemed to be immune to the law and order that characterized other parts of the nation, and that lawlessness gave rise to some of the nation's most intriguing historical figures.

Though it continued to have an economy based on cotton, lumber, oil, and ranching right up until World War II, there was still untapped potential for more. This potential would not escape notice by American leaders as the Cold War started to significantly shift the relationship between the US and other nations, particularly the Soviet Union. Houston became one of the most well-known cities in Texas when it was chosen to be home to NASA's Manned Spacecraft Center. This facility was instrumental in the early development of NASA and the space program, especially as the US and USSR engaged in the space race.

Today, the Texas economy is based on a range of different industries, particularly tourism. The extensive history of this unique state leaves little mystery as to why it attracts so much attention globally. Millions of people visit every year for many different reasons. Whether they want to see Fort Worth and the Alamo, visit the hip city of Austin, or attend space camp, there are a myriad of things to see and do in this vast landscape. If Texas were to successfully become its own nation again, it would rank 10th among the international economies in the world.

Chapter 1 – Before Columbus

Much of the history of the Americas taught in schools today focuses on how life changed following the arrival of Europeans. When Columbus first made landfall and the conquistadors began to explore the territory, all the land now known as Texas already had an ancient history filled with various rich cultures. While much of this history was lost because it was largely kept through oral traditions (much like the stories of Gilgamesh and other European tales prior to the rise of Rome), there are still many stories that have managed to survive the exploitation and genocide committed against the indigenous people in North America.

Often, Native Americans are lumped together as a homogenous group and thought of as similar in culture and religion. This is erroneous. Just as the people of Europe cannot be thrown together into a single category, thinking of all indigenous nations in the Americas as a monolith is an incredibly inaccurate depiction of what any of these people and cultures were like. North America is much larger than Europe; therefore, there was greater diversity among the Native American nations than among European countries during the 15th and 16th centuries. With the diverse environments in Texas, there was a wealth of different tribes with a wide range of cultures that had existed for centuries before the Spanish and Portuguese began to explore the land.

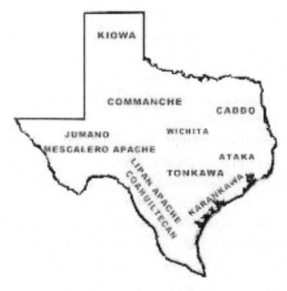

Locations of Major Native American Tribes in Texas
(*Source: https://tshaonline.org/handbook/*
online/articles/bma33)

The Caddo and the Origin of the Name "Texas"

One of the most remarkable tribes that the Spanish encountered were the Caddo. It was from the Caddo language that the region would eventually derive its name. When the Spanish spoke with the native peoples, the Caddo used the term "tashya," which meant ally or friend. The Spanish would eventually spell the word "tejas" or "texas" (pronounced tay-hass), which would be changed to Texas in English.

The Caddo people largely made their home between the Red River and Eastern Texas, though they had originally lived in an area that covered what is today the states of Arkansas, Louisiana, and

Oklahoma. Their homes were spread over a large portion of the northeastern part of Texas, and they were divided into twenty-five groups. These groups not only shared a language (Caddo) and customs but were also held together by a large confederation called the Hasinai alliance. Their customs and traditions were well established, and by the arrival of the Spanish and later the French, they would be respected for both their military prowess and artisanal skills.

What intrigued the Spanish and French most seemed to be how adept the Caddo were at trading. They did not differentiate between the different European groups (as the European groups did not differentiate between the many different Native American tribes). Spain and France eventually fought each other for the Caddo lands, and both wanted the Caddo on their side, which put the people in the Hasinai alliance in a precarious position. While they established trade with many other native peoples, this courting by the Spanish and French meant that a higher percentage of Europeans and their goods would flow through the Caddo lands. European illnesses would eventually kill as much as 95% of the Caddo people. The remaining people would eventually move to what today is Caddo County, Oklahoma.

The Fierce Apaches

Perhaps the most recognizable tribe in Texas were the Apache, an indigenous people that earned a reputation for being ferocious and fierce warriors who were far less inclined to simply accept the Europeans when they arrived. The term "Apache" includes many sub-nations, with the two largest groups in Texas being the Lipan and Mescalero. The name by which they are known today came from the Zuni language. In that language, "apachu" means enemy. Alternatively, the name could have come from the word "Awa'tehe" from the Ute language, although most sources cite the Zuni word.

The Apache gained their reputation for being fierce in battle in part because of their skills on horseback. They were the first people to acquire and use horses from the Spanish, and horses allowed them to travel much more quickly and easily. With the taming of horses, they began to live a more nomadic life than some of the other tribes in the region, which in turn allowed them to expand their trade and reach the southern part of the US. It is the use of horses as part of their regular lives that helped to make this one tribe such a familiar name in American history and lore. They traded with tribes in much more distant lands than their neighbors could, even acquiring obsidian and shells from as far away as the Pacific coast.

The Apache's culture and social structures were family-based. Males were always the leaders of the tribes, while the women shaped the tribal way of life. The men moved in with their wives after marriage, becoming members of the wife's family, even if she preceded him in death. When a wife died before her husband, her family would often help to find their son-in-law a new wife.

Hunting buffalo was one of the primary activities of the men, and tribes tended to follow the buffalo herds. Until the end of the 17th century, this was done on foot, but with the arrival of horses, the Apache could travel much further after their prey.

They were not always the fierce warriors they were portrayed to be. When the Spanish arrived and wanted to build missions, the Apache eventually agreed to help. The Lipan Apache helped to build missions and farm the land, although they largely ignored the attempts of the missionaries to convert them to Roman Catholicism. In return, the Spanish helped protect the Lipan Apache from the Comanche and Kiowa tribes. However, when the missionaries realized that the native people were still practicing their own religions, the tensions between the two groups began to grow. The missionaries began to demand more work from the Apaches and increasingly insisted they convert to Christianity. As the demands grew, the Lipan Apache eventually made the decision to leave the area. This decision was further reinforced by the missionaries' inability to supply enough food to meet the needs of the Apache, considering the amount of work that was required of them daily. Consequently, the Apache left and spread further west across Texas and Mexico.

The Comanche

The Comanche had an empire that spanned across a large swath of modern-day Texas. It is thought that they originally came from a region in Wyoming near the Platte River and had once been a part of the Eastern Shoshone. It is uncertain when they migrated south, but they formed their own tribe and, over time, gained control over a large part of the Texas region. They were one of the primary tribes in the north by the time the Spanish arrived. Shoshone who wanted to leave would often join the Comanche, growing the tribe over time.

As with the Apache, hunting bison was a large part of the Comanche's lives, and they were adept at hunting. The Comanche were more aggressive than many of the other local tribes, and it is generally thought that they stopped the Spanish from expanding further north. Like the Apache, they were skilled on horseback and knew the expansive landscape well, which made them incredibly difficult to fight. The Comanche took captives, and what befell those captives largely varied based on gender and the situation in which they were taken. Women would often be incorporated into the tribe and married off to the warriors. Many captives of both genders were often enslaved for a few years, if not for the rest of their lives.

Unlike other tribes in the region, Comanche formed no single nation or alliance. Instead, they were divided into independent groups that had the same culture and language. They would sometimes fight amongst themselves, but they largely focused on attacking their neighbors. While the Caddo, Apache, and other tribes had skilled craftspeople, the Comanche preferred to steal crafted items instead of making them.

The Comanche would prove to be the single most dangerous tribe to Americans who settled in or near their lands. Unlike many of the other tribes, the Comanche were not as accepting of the colonizers who invaded their lands and constantly fought to push them back east. The Comanche certainly earned their reputation as ferocious warriors, but the reason for their ferocity is understandable. The Comanche never agreed to any of the European colonizers attempting to lay claim to their lands, and the Americans were the first to try to steal their lands outright and settle on them, which precipitated many fierce battles. Like the Caddo, it was ultimately the arrival of European illnesses that would decimate their numbers. With their numbers reduced to just around 7,000 and many of those already on reservations by the 1870s, they could no longer fight for their lands. During the decade of the 1870s-1880s, the remaining Comanche people were moved onto reservations away from their tribal homelands.

Chapter 2 – Early Colonizers – Spain and France

When Columbus reached the Caribbean islands in 1492, it was only a matter of time before European nations came to explore "new" lands that they considered to be unowned. The Spanish were the first to arrive in Texas, but the French also explored the area in the coming years. The two nations would eventually fight over who would have control of this rich territory. It became one of many places where the European imperial rivalries would result in bloody battles.

The international fight between Spain and France would play out at the end of the 17th century. While Spain had arrived much earlier than France, France claimed a much larger portion of the continent. Both felt that the land belonged to them, though their interests in the land were very different. France was looking to establish settlements as England had along the coast. Spain feared that France was interested in attacking Mexico City and taking the gold that the Spanish conquistadors had found. The northern region was a buffer that kept them safe. By the time the fight between the two nations was over, most of North America had been divided between them.

However, the warring countries failed to account for the growing power of Great Britain.

Spain's Initial Journey from the Gulf of Mexico to the Pacific Ocean

Spanish explorers first glimpsed the lands that are part of today's Texas back in 1519 when Alonso Álvarez de Pineda mapped the coast. Pineda was the first European to explore the Gulf of Mexico. Nearly a decade later, in 1528, Pánfilo de Narváez and Álvar Núñez Cabeza de Vaca left Spain to do a more intense exploration of the lands beyond the coast. Many of the initial explorers on this trip died. Cabeza de Vaca reached land with less than ninety men on his vessel, and they were shipwrecked near what today is called Galveston Island. His ship included Estevanico, an African who had been enslaved. Estevanico is thought to have been the first person of direct African descent to have reached North America. The Karankawa tribe in the area took pity on the shipwrecked Spaniards, giving them food and shelter. Despite the aid of the native peoples, only fifteen of de Vaca's eighty men survived the winter.

Cabeza de Vaca and his remaining men would continue their quest to learn more about the land, spending eight years moving across the vast area in the southern region of North America. They did not take a straight path but followed a somewhat circuitous route, first going south before heading almost directly north. He and his small group made their way across the land largely unhampered by the native peoples, who did not see such a small party as a threat. Working as both a healer and a trader, de Vaca traveled across Texas, trying to reach Mexico City. During his initial trip south, de Vaca and his men encountered three other members of the original expedition who had been separated from them by the shipwreck. The three men had been enslaved by one of the native tribes, believed to have been the Mariames. Cabeza de Vaca was also taken prisoner, and he would remain a prisoner for several years.

Cabeza de Vaca and his three men would finally escape the Mariames roughly six years since their expedition had begun, though exact dates are not certain. The men escaped individually but met up after their escape. The Spaniards encountered the Avavares tribe as they were trying to get out of the region, and the Avavares took them in and helped them recover. It took the four men eight months to regain their health from their time in enslavement and escape.

Once able to travel, de Vaca and his men traversed west until they were close to the Pacific Ocean. As they reached the coast, they headed south. Mexico City was already well-established, and he knew that if he could make it there, he and his men would be able to safely return to Spain. It took them about two years after their escape to reach their destination. After making it to Mexico City, the Spanish explorers quickly spread the word of more riches further north.

Map 4: Overview of the Transcontinental Journey

Map of Spanish Exploration

(*Source: https://www.thestoryoftexas.com/discover/
campfire-stories/conquistadors*)

The rumors of more wealth made the Spanish believe that they could profit by plundering North America as they had Central and South America. It would take them about seventy years to realize that de Vaca and his men had been very much mistaken about what kind of riches could be found to the north.

A Misguided Hunt for Gold

As we know today, there is gold in North America but not nearly in the quantities that were present in Central and South America. Based on the rumors spread by de Vaca and his men, Spain would perpetually send explorers north to hunt for these riches. Initially, they believed the rumors because of the success of Francisco Vásquez de Coronado in modern-day New Mexico.

Based on those rumors, Coronado marched north with over 1,000 men in 1540. It took them about two and a half months before they reached something promising in the form of the Hawikuh Zuni pueblo. The streets were not lined with gold as Coronado's expedition expected, but he decided to claim the city of sandstone and adobe for Spain anyway. After reading the *Requerimiento* to the Zunis, he expected them to submit to Spanish rule and convert to Christianity. Naturally, the Zunis reacted by firing arrows at the invaders. The barbaric Spaniards entered the city and slaughtered most of the 500 people who lived there.

Feeling emboldened by the brutal and unjustified massacre, Coronado felt certain that they would find success if they kept marching and slaughtering all the native peoples who stood between them and riches. They turned east toward the Quivira Kingdom, believing that wealth was not far from their grasp. Of course, after crossing the Texas Panhandle, Coronado found absolutely nothing like he was expecting.

Though he successfully taught native peoples the dangers of Europeans, Coronado's expedition had been an utter failure in all other ways. When he returned home with less than he had when he left Mexico City, others became less inclined to journey north, as it was clear that they would not easily find the gold they wanted.

Ironically, as Coronado was heading back to Mexico City emptyhanded, Luis de Moscoso de Alvarado accidentally stumbled into modern-day Texas from the eastern side. Hernando de Soto and his men, including Alvarado, had explored Florida searching for the same gold that they simply would never find in the region. De Soto died from an illness during the spring of 1542, which left Alvarado less inclined to continue the hunt for riches, and he marched instead to Mexico City. They raided and plundered the Caddo people as they trekked west, teaching native people on the other end of the state the brutality and uncivilized methods used by Europeans to get what they wanted. Seeking to rid themselves of the vicious Spanish, one of the Caddo chiefs had his men guide Alvarado to a region with far fewer resources. When Alvarado realized what had been done, he had the guides killed. The Spanish headed down the Mississippi River to the Gulf of Mexico, reaching Mexico in the fall of 1542. His arrival confirmed what Coronado had already discovered earlier in the year: there were no riches to the north.

After dual warnings of no wealth, the only reason the Spanish went north over the next seventy years was to recover men who had gone missing. These explorers accepted assistance from the natives who were willing to help them, particularly the Jumano. Antonio de Espejo led one such expedition to find missing men, and he took a much more scholarly approach to the endeavor. He documented the trip, detailing the many different landscapes and tribes that they encountered. The Jumano provided many of the details for his journal. However, based on Espejo's findings, the Spanish in Mexico had no desire to explore further because they were only interested in wealth.

It wasn't until 1598 that the Spanish would again decide to do something in the northern regions. Juan de Oñate was tasked with establishing a settlement in what is currently New Mexico. He still harbored hope that he would get rich and was disappointed when he also discovered that there was no gold or silver paving any of the lands he visited. He claimed the modern-day El Paso region for Spain, but he didn't stay and settle as he had been ordered to do. What Oñate did find was a trade route that was well-established by the native peoples, and Spain would begin to use it to get the supplies that they did not have in Mexico City. Apart from trade, Spain did very little with the northern regions they had claimed. At the time, they believed that the lands were theirs and that there was no reason to further press their claim because no other European nations appeared interested in them.

France Seeks to Settle along the Mississippi River

France had been exploring North America during the 17th century, looking for something much different than what the Spanish desired. Like the British, the French were hoping to get rich from what they could produce in the region, not by what they could plunder from cities. In 1685, France finally made a move that the Spanish took note of: they tried to settle along the Mississippi River. At the time, the Spanish had laid claim to much of the territory between Florida and Texas, so they saw this as a move against them, particularly as it would divide Spanish contact with Florida.

René Robert Cavalier, Sieur de la Salle left France in 1684 to set up a new settlement. England had settlements in the "new world," so France wanted to claim some of the fertile regions in the south. The explorer and his crew managed to miss the Mississippi River, landing in a region that today is part of Texas, a region that the Spanish definitely believed they owned by 1685. Spain knew that the French were coming and were upset when the French settlers landed on their turf. Starting in 1686, the Spanish sent explorers into Texas and would continue to send a total of nine expeditions until 1691 to find where the French had settled. They only found a few surviving settlers, and many of the French went back to Mexico City after giving up on the settlement.

France wouldn't try to settle the region again until 1699. This time, the settlements were successful, and France managed to settle several areas between the eastern coast of Tejas and what is now modern-day New Orleans. By this point, Spain had already given up trying to settle the regions because of a series of misfortunes, including flooding and Native American aggression against them.

Chapter 3 – Spanish Settlers Claim the Region

Spanish missionaries and other religious figures had moved into the northern regions of the Americas, including parts of Texas, and managed to establish friendly relationships with the natives, including the Caddo people who had given the region its name. For a few hundred years, they and soldiers would be the only Spanish citizens who would brave the region. However, the relationship quickly soured as the Spanish gave the native peoples many reasons to distrust them, including forced labor, cheating on trade agreements, and other actions that the conquistadors became notorious for committing against native peoples in the Americas. The native peoples had also noticed by this point how unhygienic the Europeans were and how many plagues and diseases seemed to follow them, killing the indigenous who had no immunities to European illnesses. Nor was the relationship between the monks and the soldiers particularly good. They each had their own set of rules: one group followed the rules of the Spanish government and the other followed the rules of the church.

Tribes like the Apache would eventually leave, but the Spanish had established a foothold in several different parts of Texas. As

France and England had growing settlements on the continent, these Texan regions became more important to Spain because they provided protection for the larger Spanish settlements in the Central and South American regions. After successfully removing the French from the region, Spain wanted to ensure that they did not lose any land to other empires. The Spanish then founded San Antonio in 1718 to dissuade other European nations from moving further west.

The First Governor and Eastern Settlements

While most of the Spanish explorers didn't have much interest in the region north of Mexico City, Spanish members of the Roman Catholic Church saw potential. By the early 1700s, the Spanish Crown had realized the threat posed by the French, and, to deter them from trying to settle in lands that the Spanish had claimed, the Spanish Crown decided to designate a governor of the region. The first person to be appointed to the post was General Domingo Terán de los Rios. He was charged with managing Coahuila, Texas, and the surrounding area. He focused on establishing settlements to the east near the area where the French had tried to build their first settlement. Monks of the Franciscan order first moved east with the Spanish soldiers to help establish these settlements. The soldiers were meant to protect the settlement and guard the land, while the Franciscan priests would build missions and convert the local populations to the east. New missions were formed near the Rio Grande and then into western Texas as the settlements proved to be beneficial, if not enriching, to Spain.

The settlements were called presidios (fortifications), and they were fortified to ensure that the settlers were safe. These were primarily where the soldiers and other settlers lived, and the walls provided a place for secular needs, such as enforcing laws and housing soldiers. The Franciscans had their own establishments in the missions they built. Both missions and presidios were built in the same area, and they worked together (similar to how churches, courthouses, and other government buildings were often the central buildings in new towns in American settlements about 100 years later).

The Franciscans were not required to follow the laws of the soldiers and other civilians. They had their own laws based on the Roman Catholic Church, which were above the laws of the non-clergy. This resulted in tensions between the missions and the presidios, mostly because the Franciscans often decried the abuses their countrymen perpetrated against the native peoples. The abuses of the secular Spanish went against the teachings of the priests, and it made their attempts to convert natives considerably more difficult. The secular settlers resented the fact that the Franciscans did not have to follow their laws. They were equally upset with the frequency with which the Franciscans would oppose their attempts to rule over the native peoples. Technically, the newly converted people were part of the missions, not the presidios. This went against everything that the Spanish had been doing since their arrival in the New World, and they believed that the religious men were undermining their efforts to control the population.

The Spanish monarchy did not intercede in these squabbles because it did not have the same goals or interests as the settlers. To the Spanish government, the settlements were simply a buffer against any encroachment on their lands that could result in loss of the gold they were still seeking in the lands further south.

The First Settlements

The Franciscans largely decided where settlements would be built because they were primarily interested in occupying the lands. They saw the native people as potential converts, which was a much greater form of wealth to them than gold. The first successful settlements during the 1680s were in San Angelo, El Paso, and Presidio, all in the area that is currently New Mexico. As they then began to work to create the buffer zone in the eastern portion of the region, the first real Texas towns were established. The very first was in what is now San Antonio. They also established a settlement in an area that had been abandoned by the Caddo, a place called Nacogdoches. Missions began to try to integrate with the native populations, most notably the Apache. However, none of these missions lasted for long, and the native peoples usually were not sincere in their conversion. Their interest lay more in how the Spanish could protect them from aggressive tribes than in forgoing their deities and religions.

While many of the settlements did not last, the buildings that were made during this time were incredibly durable. Among the most famous buildings made during the period of Spanish missionary settlements was the Alamo. However, these settlements were not made to be protective; they were made to be convenient places for gatherings and for the missionaries to work with the native peoples. These settlements were largely open and inviting, though some military fortifications were added since soldiers were present as well. The fortifications were made to protect the Spanish and their native allies against other hostile native tribes. Considering these tribes used less advanced weapons, the settlements did not need the kind of robust protection as the regions near other European settlers.

Rising Concerns Following the Louisiana Purchase

Spain and its colonies thought they had a decent buffer established against the French. After all, the French did not have many settlements in the region, and it was easy to ensure that they did not encroach on the Spanish lands. In 1803, Spain became very concerned with the future of its territory in North America when the French sold a large percentage of the lands claimed by France to the young United States. Suddenly, there was a much larger, more immediate threat to the Spanish territory. Americans were not only much closer but also more numerous on the continent. It was only a matter of time before American settlers moved west to explore their new acquisition from the French. There was no guarantee that the settlers would know which lands were theirs and which belonged to Spain.

Perhaps of greater concern was the fact that the region of Texas had never been well-defined. Initially, Spain and the US tried to avoid problems by establishing a fifty-mile wide neutral area. Despite this effort to keep the peace, tensions were not eased. Spain had reason to be concerned because of the American's growing belief in Manifest Destiny. After the young nation had acquired such an expansive region, it began to believe its God-given destiny was to rule over all the land between the Atlantic and Pacific Oceans. This was not a well-formed idea initially because the Americans did not have any knowledge of those lands. However, more the Americans explored and learned more, there was a growing, though unfounded, belief that they were destined to incorporate most of North American into their nation. This meant obtaining the lands controlled by Spain.

Ironically, Spain would try to solve its problem by inviting Americans to settle in their territory. The Americans would end up being less of a problem for Spain than it had anticipated, as it was the Spanish settlers who would ultimately rebel against them. Just seven years after the Louisiana Purchase, the War for Mexican Independence began. Spain lost interest in the actions of the American settlers in Texas because they stood to lose a lot more as their people in Mexico rebelled. Texas had always been viewed as simply a buffer area to protect the lands that were now demanding independence from Spain. Spain's primary concern from 1810 on would be retaining its colonies rather than stemming the flood of American settlers, whom it would invite into the region in just a few years as the Mexican War for Independence dragged on.

Chapter 4 – Americans Settle

Realizing that they couldn't possibly colonize all their new land, the Spanish decided the best way to make the most of those lands was to invite the Americans to come and settle. Americans had been profiting off the land across North America for a few centuries by this point, something the Spanish hadn't genuinely attempted to do. Starting in 1820, Spain invited their northern neighbors to settle, with a few stipulations. This invitation was extended despite the political upheaval in the area—Spain's hold over Mexico was precarious, at best.

When the War for Mexican Independence ended, the new Mexican government had to decide whether to honor the invitation that Spain had extended. Any Americans who had made an agreement with Spain would now also need to make a similar agreement with the new Mexican government before they would be able to settle. This was complicated by the arrival of Americans in Texas prior to the war's end. Ultimately, Mexico would allow the settlers to stay and continue to allow new settlers into the region if they met similar conditions to those that were set by Spain.

Successful Settlements Prior to the American Settlements

Despite numerous attempts by the Spanish missionaries and soldiers to create viable areas to live, by 1820, there were only three established Texas settlements: La Bahía del Espíritu Santo (which would later become Goliad), Nacogdoches, and San Antonio de Bexar. These settlements were small towns that had a few ranches dotting the area around them.

One of the primary reasons that so many of their other attempts failed was the increasing hostility of Comanche and Kiowa, who did not like the Spaniards invading their territory. Unlike the Caddo and Apache, the Comanche and Kiowa saw no benefit in allowing the Spanish to have footholds in lands that their tribes had occupied for generations, especially because the Spanish had made it clear that they considered themselves superior. Despite this Spanish belief of superiority, the Native Americans were easily able to destroy or to accelerate the failure of several settlements.

The religious laws that had ruled when the three successful settlements were established were largely abandoned by this time, and the mission in Nacogdoches had been closed before the end of the 18th century. As the settlements became more secular, there was increasingly more reason to allow others to take on the incredibly difficult task of creating settlements on Native land. Spain was more accustomed to taking over settled areas, not in creating safe havens in open terrain. Americans had already proven to be very adept at turning "untamed" lands into profitable towns. Spain hoped to profit from this ingenuity without having to do much more than offer Americans land.

Conditions for Settling in Texas

Though the Spanish had positioned themselves to bar European countries from their lands, they took a different approach with their northern neighbors. During the last years of the 18th century, Spain had invited Americans to settle in their lands near Upper Louisiana. Using the offer they had made during that time as a template, Spain tried to lure Americans further west. In exchange for land in Texas, Americans would need to

agree to three requirements.

Spain had long been a proponent of the Roman Catholic Church, while most of the US was Protestant. These were considered incompatible, so one of the most important stipulations the Spanish made was that any Americans settling in their lands convert to Roman Catholicism. Almost as important was the second stipulation that the American settlers would be loyal to Spain, not the US. This meant that they would need to renounce their American citizenship and become Spanish citizens. However, American settlers would not have the same rights as people who were born Spanish citizens. This inequality was not obvious, and if the settlers realized it, they likely decided that it wouldn't matter much since they would be living far away from the large Spanish settlements. To protect their investment, Spain also insisted that the American settlers primarily trade with them instead of the US. It was a calculated risk that the Spanish hoped would boost their economy, especially during the war for Mexican Independence.

Empresarios (as potential settlers were called) could request a grant from Spain, and if approved, they would be able to establish their settlements. The empresarios would be responsible for the people who settled under their agreement, a stipulation that Mexico would also adopt when they later made agreements with the empresarios.

Americans were more than happy to agree to the conditions in exchange for inexpensive land. The cost of land in the US was $1.25 per acre, and they were required to buy at least eighty acres for a total of $100. Spain was offering the head of a family (whether a man or a woman) 4,605 acres for only $184, which could be paid over a six-year period instead of all at once. This attracted the attention of scores of Americans who sought to make their own fortunes.

Another reason so many Americans were willing to move was that they expected the US to eventually purchase the region from Spain. By this time, Manifest Destiny was a belief shared by many Americans, though neither Spain nor Mexico would understand that this belief also applied to them and not just to the native peoples. Had the Spanish realized that Americans expected to take over the whole region, they likely would have taken the same protective stance against Americans as they had against the French, instead of openly inviting Americans onto the northern lands of Mexico.

Finally, there were Americans who were fleeing from the law and deportation, the most notable of which was the Austin family. Though Stephen Austin's father, Moses Austin, had brokered a deal with Spain to settle 300 people in Texas, he died before the settlers reached their destination. It was left to Stephen to make a new agreement with Mexico for the settlers. He renegotiated for the group, but nothing was mentioned about criminals and debtors. Without an agreement between the US and Mexico to extradite criminals, Texas could be a haven for many people who were in financial trouble and had opted to move west to avoid debt collectors and the law.

A Change in Government

Mexico won its independence in 1821. Among the many things they needed to establish was how to deal with the Americans who had made agreements with Spain to settle Texas. While those agreements were now void because Spain no longer had any power in the region, several empresarios (the most well-known of which was Stephen Austin) were planning to move hundreds of Americans into the region.

Mexico agreed to renegotiate the terms of the agreements, largely keeping things the same. One notable difference was that settlers need only profess that they were Christian, not specifically Roman Catholic. The predominant religion in Mexico was Catholic, and it was likely implied that the settlers should become Catholic. However, they avoided specifying that the settlers would need to convert. They further made it clear that the settlers' religion was not a primary concern: they did not even provide a priest for any of the settlements until 1831. This meant that many of the Americans could not complete basic religious ceremonies. Most notably, they could not marry without a priest present. Many resorted to establishing marriage bonds and then making them official when the priest finally arrived.

Though Austin was the first empresario, Mexico would go on to make individual agreements with about thirty empresarios, resulting in the arrival of about 9,000 families. Initially, Austin only had 300 settlers. Each empresario had their own agreement with a set number of people they could bring to the region. This was how Mexico attempted to control the number of Americans that settled on their lands. All the contracts clearly defined where the settlers were permitted to establish their new homes and how much land each family could have. The empresarios always got more than the people who came along with them, but, with so much land available, settlers usually accepted the disparity in land distribution. All contracts were six years long, during which time settlers would have to pay for their land. Payments were usually based on what they had earned from the land. The last contractual settlement was with the Mercer colony, signed in January 1844.

A Question of How to Handle Slaves

Slavery had been one of the primary reasons that the farmers and plantations in the US had been successful. Spain and Mexico both knew that the Americans would not come without slaves to prop up their settlements. Though both Spain and Mexico did not want slavery in their lands, they were willing to allow the first settlers to bring slaves so that the Americans could be financially successful. Mexico hoped to benefit financially, in turn.

Slaves were not allowed to be sold in Texas, but initially, settlers were permitted to bring slaves they already owned. Once in Texas, settlers could buy and sell or trade slaves among themselves, though new slaves were not permitted to be brought in specifically for selling. This agreement stood until 1840. However, some officials signaled their unwillingness to allow slavery to continue for much longer in the settlements. It was hinted as early as 1827 that the practice of slavery would be ended and slaves emancipated at some point. In response, slave owners set up indentured servant contracts with their illiterate slaves that tied the slaves to them for ninety-nine years, essentially keeping Mexico from being able to emancipate them.

Mexican officials were not pleased with this move, but they did not do anything to stop it. The most forceful step to stop slavery in Texas came from President Vicente Ramón Guerrero, who declared emancipation in September 1829. Several of the empresarios quickly deployed to Mexico City to try to get an exemption from the emancipation.

The question of slavery would be as much a point of contention between American settlers and Mexico as it was between the northern and southern states in the US.

Stephen Austin and the Formation of the Texas Rangers

As the first empresario, Austin had much more autonomy and control than subsequent empresarios. His negotiations with Mexico would often be implemented across other settlements. With little to no support from Mexico, Austin was responsible for those who wanted to immigrate into the land Mexico had allowed him to settle. The Mexican government did not want too many foreigners populating their lands, but they also did not have the capability to provide any legal assistance or protection to the incoming people.

The burden of creating and enforcing law and order and distributing land, as well as creating all the settlement's social infrastructure—such as roads, schools, granaries, and sawmills—fell on Austin.

Perhaps the most difficult job Austin had was dealing with the Mexican government, though. Mexico was not able to help the settlers but still expected the settlers to follow Mexican laws. This included a ban on slaves, which the American settlers refused to relinquish. Despite the desire to keep all people marginally free in Mexico, Austin negotiated for the Americans' ability to keep their slaves after the Mexican government banned the institution in 1829.

With criminals coming to the area to escape the laws in the US and Native Americans fighting to keep the settlers off their lands, Austin decided that he needed to form a group that could both protect the settlers and provide law enforcement. While Austin was in Mexico City working to safeguard the rights to continued settlement, one of his lieutenants, Moses Morrison, formed a militia to protect the settlers. The militia consisted of ten men who swore to rise to the occasion when needed. Morrison assembled this small contingent to go to the Texas coast, where the Karankawa and Tonkawa tribes were continually attacking the settlers.

When Austin returned from Mexico, he doubled the number of men to twenty, all of them paid volunteers. Each volunteer was offered fifteen dollars a month, though the payment was often in land instead of money. In the early days, the men were called for a variety of different needs, and the militia was not permanent. When their services were not needed, the volunteers would be disbanded so that they could care for their families. The first volunteers consisted of a very diverse range of individuals, including Hispanics, Anglos, and Native Americans. The combined talents of these individuals made a highly effective volunteer militia. These twenty men would be the first members of the organization that would come to be known as the Texas Rangers.

Chapter 5 – Rising Tensions between Mexico and the Settlements

Resentment between American settlers and the Mexican government grew quickly after the settlements were established. The settlers had been dissatisfied with the agreements that they had made with Mexico, particularly the stipulation that they would eventually have to give up their slaves. Mexico began to resent how many of the American settlers were completely disregarding the agreements that they had made. The empresarios were not controlling the flow of immigrants into the region, and consequently, Mexico was losing its grip on large swaths of Texas land.

The expectation that the Americans would be grateful for the land and would agree to live by Mexican laws proved to be a serious miscalculation. The more control Mexico tried to exert over their territories, the more resentful the Americans became. After all, the Americans had established their own way of life largely without Mexican assistance. The Texas Rangers had been formed to protect American settlers because the Mexican government could not spare the men to protect them, and Americans in the region had become accustomed to enforcing their own laws. The idea that Mexico expected them to abide by their agreements seemed incomprehensible to the Americans, who disregarded the few requirements they were given in exchange for a new life and a lot of land.

The Effects of the Mexican War of Independence

Having won their independence from Spain, Mexico had hoped that the settlers would be able to turn the lands into something profitable. Like the Spanish before them, the Mexicans did not want to extend the same rights to the settlers that their native-born enjoyed. Americans were considered inferior to the people in power, who were largely wealthy former Spaniards. With both sides viewing each other as inferior people, it was only a matter of time before these views caused more serious problems.

Mexico had won its independence at a very high cost both in terms of lives and resources, and the new country was facing serious financial devastation when the war ended in 1821. The mines that had once produced a considerable amount of money under Spanish control were not nearly as efficient under the new government. Food production was also significantly reduced as Mexicans sought to earn more money through other endeavors. Unemployment was another significant problem; there was not enough money in circulation to pay workers, which further drove people to emigrate in the hopes of finding work and a livelihood. Unrest and other serious problems were further exacerbated by the large class disparity within the fledgling country.

The settlements had become accustomed to the laisse faire approach that the Mexican people took toward the settlements. Of course, Mexico couldn't provide much support, but it also meant that they didn't interfere in the way settlements were run. The empresarios were pretty much their governmental leaders, or at least that was largely how they saw it. However, once the Mexican government was formed, it expected that the settlers would begin to heed its demands. This diverse view of the role of the Mexican government in the settlers' lives was further complicated by the kind of people who became the leaders of the new Mexican government. Those who rose to leadership within the Mexican government had very little experience in governing; they were not prepared to deal with the rising problems. This led to the wealthy, religious figures, and military leaders stepping into more prominent roles to retain the class structure that had existed under Spanish rule. While they had wanted freedom from Spain, most of the people in these three social groups did not want equality. By ensuring that the antebellum order continued in the new country, the gentry, church officials, and military leaders would have equal control over the direction of the government—much more than they would have enjoyed had Spain continued to control the region. To all the powerful parties in Mexico, the American settlers seemed to be a perfect solution to some of their problems: they would help improve the financial situation in Mexico while protecting the country from further US expansion.

Settlers had long been dealing with a problem that the former Spanish citizens had not—they had survived amid the constant attacks of the native peoples in the north. The lands were populated with Native Americans who were not welcoming of invaders, and they did not recognize Mexico as owners of their ancestral homelands (just as they had not acknowledged the theft of these lands by Spain). Mexico had too many problems to contend with to quell the threat that the native peoples posed. By leaving the settlers to contend with the Native Americans, Mexico wouldn't have to worry about being attacked by those groups. They had enough problems in Mexico City as different factions tried to take control of the government to contend with the issues posed by the northern regions. Essentially, Mexico hoped the settlers would distract the native population, making the native peoples an American problem. Even as the settlers slaughtered the natives that Mexico could not fight, the Mexicans somehow thought that they would be better able to control the Americans than they had the natives. This would quickly prove to be untrue.

In 1824, Mexico passed a national colonization law, intended to supersede the older imperial colonization law, and it changed the way the Mexican territory would be populated and governed. Instead of dealing with the Mexican government directly, people wishing to establish new contracts to settle in the territory would need to go to the state legislatures. Many of the states hoped they could have greater control over themselves and attempted to mimic how the US states largely self-governed, with minimal interference from the federal government. While the 1824 Federal Constitution of the United Mexican States took much of its inspiration from the Constitution of the United States of America, it also included some of the tenets that had been written in the Spanish Constitution of 1812. This change would prove to be significant, as the states were better able to monitor the settlers than the Mexican federal government had. They also took a greater interest in who was settling their lands.

Two of the main states located in the northern region were Texas and Coahuila. Ultimately, both would become a part the American state called Texas, but during the 18th century, they were separate. Under the jurisdiction of Nuevo Santander, both territories had their own missions, but in 1716, they were governed by Martin de Alarcon.

Map of Texas and Coahuila
(*Source:https://commons.wikimedia.org/wiki/File:Hooker_Map_of_t
he_State_of_Coahuila
_and_Texas_1834_UTA.jpg*)

Implementing the New Mexican Laws

Following the passing of the new law, government leaders met in Saltillo, the capital of the Mexican state of Coahuila, to establish the rules for determining who could settle the northern lands and what requirements must be followed. The officials in Saltillo would set the requirements and define the terms of any agreement with empresarios in Texas, which meant that they would also determine who would receive the contracts, whether the applicants were American, European, or Mexican. These rules were documented in the state colonization law.

The focus of the government leaders was largely on ranching and farming to produce more food and encourage the growth of commerce in the region among the different settlements. According to the new law, Mexicans would have the first choice of land in settling the northern region; then, Americans would be allowed to settle. Although they would be required to pay for the land where they settled, initially immigrants would not be taxed as they strove to establish themselves. All they needed to do was agree to be bound by the contract their empresario had signed and take an oath that they would abide by its requirements, including becoming Mexican citizens. Once the oath was completed, settlers became naturalized Mexicans.

Problems arose when the federal government realized how much the settlers were neglecting the oath they had taken. Many of the Americans were failing to live up to the few requirements of the oath, retaining their own traditions instead of integrating with the Mexican traditions and people. More egregiously, Americans did not adopt Mexican laws in their settlements. They blatantly disregarded the laws that were inconvenient to their way of life and implemented their own local laws instead, some of which contradicted Mexican laws.

Growing Resentment

Nearly a decade before Texas instigated a war for independence, other American settlers were already expressing a desire to revolt against the Mexican government. The first such revolt was precipitated by a man named Haden Edwards. Edwards and the settlers in his colony declared independence in 1826, calling their land the Republic of Fredonia. They had planned to work with the Cherokee to form an alliance and create a new flag representing the Americans and native peoples. After signing a declaration of independence in December of 1826, they turned to the US for support. They also asked Stephen Austin to assist them in their fight against the Mexican government. Predictably, Austin sided with the Mexican government, and he joined the Mexicans in putting down the rebellion. By the end of January 1827, the Republic of Fredonia was no more. Unhappy that they had been dragged into such a poorly-planned rebellion, the Cherokee killed the main leaders, John

Dunn Hunter and Richard Fields. Haden Edwards survived by fleeing and would later return to join in the War of Texas Independence.

Mexico was understandably shaken by this apparently unprovoked call for independence and became wary of allowing any further American settlers into its territories. Since it had been the responsibility of the federal government, not the state government, to put down the rebellion, leaders of the Mexican government began to try to consolidate power. Desiring to build a much stronger central government that more closely copied the way that Spain had ruled, they began drafting new laws toward the end of 1829 and passed them in April of 1830. The new laws voided any existing agreement with the settlers if the settlers were not complying with the terms of that agreement, in addition to curtailing American immigration. The only exceptions to this were the settlements under Stephen Austin and Green DeWitt. The Mexican government found that these two empresarios had fulfilled their requirements (something that was not completely true for either of the two men). The Mexican government also established military outposts so they could prevent new American settlers from entering Mexico and Texas. No more slaves would be allowed to be brought into the country, though slaves who currently resided there would remain enslaved.

For the five years prior to the new agreement, both Coahuila and the American settlers had greatly benefited from the relationship they had established. In fact, they were prospering in a way that had eluded much of the rest of Mexico. Commerce had become stable and was even lucrative in some regions. The federal government's interference threatened both the free commerce that had been established as well as the sovereignty of Coahuila. Slaves had been allowed to be brought into Coahuila because there were not enough people to work the lands without them. However, they were now to be indentured, giving them the ability to earn money to buy their own freedom. Under the new laws, though, it would no longer be possible to bring in new slaves, and people in the Texan territory feared that this would reduce their ability to conduct commerce and simultaneously stunt growth. It was suspected that eliminating the ability to bring any more slaves into Mexico was meant to deter the kinds of Americans who often came. The Mexicans believed that if Americans could not bring their slaves, they would not be tempted to enter the country without authorization. The rise in anti-immigration laws resulted in much greater hostility between the Anglo-Americans and Mexicans and did not have the desired effect of cooling the situation. The settlers perceived this as the Mexicans interfering in the territories that were under settler control, proving that they still saw themselves as Americans, not as Mexicans. Both the resistance to follow Mexican laws and immigration requirements understandably upset the Mexican leaders.

A Mexican politician and general named Santa Anna acted in 1833 to alleviate the issue. He led the government in revoking the law that had institutionalized immigration discrimination, and the effects were nearly immediate, as Americans began to immigrate into the regions that had been prospering under the better-established settlements. Roughly a year later, Santa Anna would reverse his decision to allow greater states' rights. He called for the congregation of a new congress that would create a strong central government. It took nearly a year, but the country was reconfigured in the fall of 1835, with states being converted into departments that would then be controlled by presidential appointees.

This did not sit well with the people in Coahuila, particularly the people in Stephen Austin's settlement. Mexico was embroiled in a civil war by this time, which made it the opportune time for Texans to finally break from the nation that had invited them to settle the lands that belonged to the Native Americans.

Chapter 6 – The Fight for Texas Independence Begins

Within ten years of Mexico finally gaining its independence from Spain, Americans decided that they needed to fight to become independent from what they saw as the dictatorial control of the Mexican government. Some of the primary American empresarios, such as Stephen Austin, sought to find a peaceful resolution and ended up caught in a fight between their settlers and the Mexican government. Though it was already facing a civil war, Mexico soon found itself fighting another internal battle—this time with the very people it had hoped would help the country prosper. Almost from the beginning, the Americans made it obvious that they had no desire to integrate into their host nation's culture or respect the oaths they took when they settled in Mexican territory. As the Mexican people were preoccupied with civil war, the Americans saw their opportunity to do what they had largely expected (or in some cases intended) to happen: they sought to remove themselves from Mexican oversight and find a way to be annexed to the US.

The Final Straw

After Mexico appointed a representative to govern the regions, the American settlers— particularly those living in Coahuila—let their anger at the move be known. Up to this point, they had largely been left to their own devices. Government oversight of the nation where they lived was considered dictatorial. Ironically, the American settlers turned to another federal government that was much more hands-on, proving that their problem was more with the fact that they were supposed to become Mexican rather than remain American.

While US states did have a considerable amount of autonomy, the US federal government had much input on how things were run within the states. In fact, the struggle between states' rights and the federal role was a problem that was proving to be very much at the forefront of US consciousness at the time. But the rebellion of the American settlers in Mexico was more about the fear of losing their way of life than in any actual problem. The threat of losing their slaves was a primary concern, and the right to own slaves was something they knew that the US would preserve if they could get the US to annex their region.

Fearing the rise of the settlers against the government, particularly as the settlers became more vocal, the Mexican commander in Coahuila requested reinforcements to quell the unrest of the settlers. As word spread that a military force was being raised against them, William B. Travis led a group of Texans to attack Anahuac in June of 1835. When they refused to surrender, Mexico took this as a direct rebellion against Mexican laws. With this direct violation of the oath the settlers had taken, war was all but inevitable.

Perhaps one of the worst things that Mexico did to disenfranchise the settled Americans was to try to make an example of the person who was most loyal to Mexico. Austin had constantly insisted that the people who settled as a part of his agreement always abide by Mexican law. In return, Austin's settlement thrived and had significantly better protection than that of any other settlement, as well as large portions of Mexico. When the Mexican government decided to make an example of Austin by imprisoning him after he tried to negotiate a peaceful resolution, Mexico managed to turn its best ally against itself. After a year of imprisonment, even Stephen Austin called for an independent Texas. When Austin returned to his settlement in 1835, Texas made their move to break away from Mexico.

Open Conflict

With Austin's return after an imprisonment based on no charges, the people of Texas finally had a figurehead to lead them into a fight for independence.

The first real conflict in the fight for Texan independence was at the Battle of Gonzales in October of 1835. The fight began as a simple request that the colonists at Gonzales return a cannon that had been given to them in 1831 to help during Native American attacks. When they refused, Texas Commander Domingo de Ugartechea sent 100 soldiers to retrieve the cannon. Knowing that the tension would make the situation precarious, de Ugartechea instructed the leader, Lieutenant Francisco de Castañeda, to avoid conflict if possible, but did say that force was acceptable if necessary. On September 27, 1835, the Mexicans left San Antonio for Gonzales. After two days, they arrived at their destination only to find that they could not cross the Guadalupe River because of flooding and the presence of eighteen American militiamen. Castañeda told the eighteen men that he had a dispatch for Andrew Ponton, and he was told that the alcalde (the Spanish name for a mayor or magistrate) was not present. While Castañeda's men pitched their camp on the opposite side of the river, the people in Gonzales requested reinforcements.

A member of the Coushatta tribe made his way into the Mexican camp and informed Castañeda that the number of men in Gonzales ready to fight was 140 or more. Instead of staying put out in the open, Castañeda had the camp broken down and forded the river further away. The soldiers set up a new camp on October 1, about seven miles from their destination.

The men in Gonzales did not sit still as they saw the Mexicans leave. Crossing the river to where the Mexicans had originally made camp, they worked their way along the river until they found the new camp. On October 2, they attacked the Mexican camp. When the first round of fighting ceased, Castañeda requested a parley. The commander of the rebels was John Henry Moore, and he agreed to the parley. While he learned that Castañeda agreed with much of the ideas that the settlers had, Castaneda could not go against his orders to retrieve the cannon. When it became clear that the fighting would resume, Castaneda knew that his side could not win. Though he and his men had been attacked without provocation, he wanted to minimize the fighting. Calling for a retreat, the Mexicans returned to Commander Ugartechea.

The battle was little more than a short skirmish over the presence of a cannon, but the victory was the sign the settlers needed to help them decide it was the time to finally engage in open war. Austin was called to be the commander of the forces fighting for Texas separation, though he was not a military man. He was a diplomat, as would quickly become obvious. He was soon replaced by Sam Houston and assumed the role of envoy to the US. Austin spent most of the war trying to convince the US to intervene on behalf of Texas. His efforts failed because the US did not want to start a war with Mexico. The US was not as divided as Mexico, but it was already plagued with many internal struggles, with slavery one of the greatest concerns.

The Texas Declaration of Independence and How the Texas Rangers Earned a More Prominent Role in the New Country

Following the events at Gonzales, the settlers convened, and a consultation drafted the Texas Declaration of Independence on November 7, 1835. It was signed by fifty-nine men, three of whom were Mexican descendants. This showed that some people who had settled the region had a sense of entitlement. On some levels, this seems natural because, up to this point, the settlers had fended for themselves. However, the declaration was in direct opposition to what the settlers had agreed to when they moved to the region. Nothing that had happened was unexpected. The people knew that they would be on the frontier, making a living for themselves. The problem was that they had grown to believe that Manifest Destiny was all but guaranteed, particularly since Mexico had done little to demonstrate an interest in their settlements. The instability of the Mexican government was a serious problem, even for those of Mexican descent, so some decided to join the other settlers instead of siding with the country that had not provided them with much support.

By 1836, the Texas Revolution had begun, and it was going well for the Texans almost from the beginning. During this time, volunteers and soldiers played a major role in the victory for Texas Independence, but the Texas Rangers had an equally crucial role. As the soldiers were focused on fighting the Mexicans, the settlers were easy targets for both Native Americans and the Mexican military. This was the first recorded instance where the Texas Rangers received a government sanction to patrol the frontiers against the Native Americans. Some of the members of the Rangers also fought against the Mexican government, but most of the forces worked to protect the settlers while others fought in the war for Texan independence. As the Rangers were adept trackers, some of them were called on to act as scouts. Also, because they were familiar with the lands, others served as carriers.

After the disaster at the Alamo (in modern-day San Antonio) in March of 1836, the Rangers went to help the Texans fleeing from the area. They assisted in getting settlers to safety and destroyed anything left behind so that it could not be used by the Mexicans, including produce from the farms. When the Rangers were called to act as escorts at the Battle of San Jacinto in April of 1836, many of them were annoyed with their role. They preferred either to fight in the war against the Mexicans or against the Native Americans. The menial tasks assigned to them during the war seemed to be a step down from their usual duties, which had been important when the area was a part of Mexican Texas. However, their role began to undergo a significant shift following the close of the war, largely because they became the only established law enforcement group in Texas. How the Rangers were used by the new government varied depending on the governor in charge, but their place and role in the new country began to solidify.

Chapter 7 – "Remember the Alamo" and Other Major Battles

One of the most notorious events in US history occurred in a territory that didn't even belong to the United States, and it was an illegal attempt by some Americans to steal lands from another nation. Of course, that isn't quite the way many Americans have portrayed it. As the Americans in Texas began to feel that Mexicans were demonstrating authoritarian tendencies, some began to believe that they didn't need to continue to follow any of their agreements with the nation of Mexico.

While the Americans thought they were fighting for independence from a dictatorial government, Mexico believed that the Americans were in breach of their agreement and were stealing lands that belonged to Mexico. The War of Texas Independence was already being fought by the time the Americans tried to defend the old Spanish mission, but it was the events that happened there that provided a rallying cry against the Mexicans.

A Brief History of the Alamo

The Alamo was over 100 years old when its name became the rallying cry for Americans trying to establish their own country.

Originally founded as a mission to convert the native peoples of the area, the structure was well constructed. It was part of the established settlements in San Antonio, making it one of the oldest European structures in the region. As the chapel for the original mission, it was erected between 1716 and 1718, though it is not known when it was finished and put to use. Over the next 100 years, Spanish soldiers would stop at the Alamo to rest during their marches across the region. The soldiers were the ones to give the structure its name, the Alamo (Spanish for cottonwood), because of the number of cottonwood trees in the region.

A Flawed Plan

As the War of Texas Independence waged on, more Americans continued to enter the territory, with many of them deciding to fight in the war. Some of them made their way west toward San Antonio, despite warnings from Sam Houston, who was the leader of the Texan military forces. The American leaders had decided it was best to leave San Antonio because it was too difficult to defend, but the volunteers disregarded their warnings. By this time, the Alamo was more than 125 years old, and it had not been well maintained. The men insisted on remaining despite being exposed to the elements and the Mexican forces.

Several famous Americans were a part of the group of volunteers who refused to give up their position. The commanders of the volunteers were James Bowie and William B. Travis. Bowie is best known for the knife that was named after him. Perhaps the best-known participant in the events at the Alamo was David (Davy) Crockett, a former congressman and frontiersman. Crockett had been disillusioned by American politics, particularly President Andrew Jackson's genocide of Native Americans. Having failed to prevent the events leading up to the Trail of Tears, Crockett left the US to make a new life in Texas. All three men had experience on the frontier, but their experience did not necessarily prepare them for an actual fight against a military force, especially not an army commanded by one of the most renowned Mexican military leaders they faced in February of 1836.

Mexican General Antonio Lopez de Santa Anna had been marching with the Mexican military west to put down the settlers' rebellion. He and an army of between 1,800 and 6,000 men (records on the number of Mexican soldiers vary) arrived at the Alamo on February 23, 1836. Upon their arrival, they began a siege of the Alamo.

A Grim Realization, an Appeal for Help, and the Birth of a Rallying Cry

When the siege began, it quickly became very clear to the American volunteers that Houston had been right in his assessment of the impossibility of protecting the region. Travis acted on this realization and sent word to anyone who could be reached, pleading with "the people of Texas & all Americans in the world" to come and support them in their ill-conceived desire to keep a structure that was neither strategic for victory nor beneficial to the larger fight.

Once in position, the Mexican military began to fire cannons on the walls of the Alamo, reducing much of the outer structure to rubble. Despite the odds, the Americans did manage to hold the Alamo for thirteen days, defending it against a much greater force. The Mexicans had an equally difficult time trying to remove the Americans because the region was not ideal for fighting.

It is said that Travis sent a woman out to act as a messenger for the Texans in the Alamo. She relayed the message that they were willing to surrender if Santa Anna would agree to spare the lives of the Texans. The response was that the people in the Alamo had to surrender with no guarantee about what would happen to them. To the Mexicans, the Texans were traitors who did not deserve any kind of concession. Once they had their answer, the people in the Alamo decided that their only option was to take out as many Mexicans as they could because there was no chance of beating such a large, well-trained force.

On March 6, 1836, the Mexicans finally decided to push forward after suffering heavy casualties; they were more exposed than the Texans hiding in the Alamo. Santa Anna ordered them to storm the Alamo through a breach in the structure's wall, and they were to spare none of the defenders. It took three attempts, but the final push forward finally broke the defenders. The Mexican soldiers followed through with Santa Anna's order to kill all the defenders, sparing the lives of only women and children. Of the 180 to 260 Americans who had been at the Alamo, it is said that only fifteen survived. The number of Mexicans who died is estimated to be between 600 and 1,600. Houston had been right about how impossible it was to fight in such an open, old area, and it had been a rather ill-advised fight for either side.

With so few survivors and the loss of some of the most notable American frontiersmen at the Alamo, many Texans were enraged. When they marched into battle about a month later, Houston led a force into battle against Santa Anna to the rallying cry of "Remember the Alamo!"

The Battle of San Jacinto and the End of the Fight for Texas Independence

The defeat at the Alamo was the first of two crushing blows; the second was the Goliad Massacre. An estimated 350 rebels were killed about a month after the disaster at the Alamo. Those who were captured during the battle were executed, giving the settlers more reason to persist. If the Texans were to give up because of the defeats, they could expect a very harsh response to the rebellion.

Santa Anna saw the two Mexican victories as a sign that the Texans would soon be defeated, leading to a serious miscalculation on his part: he divided his military to try to finish off the rebels faster. Angered by the way Santa Anna had refused to take prisoners,

General Sam Houston went after the legendary Mexican military leader. The Texan finally caught up to the smaller Mexican military at the San Jacinto River on April 21, 1836. As Santa Anna had not expected the Texans to be on the offensive, the attack took him and his men by surprise. The attack became a rout, and about half of the Mexicans were killed. Santa Anna and the rest of his men were taken prisoner. As Santa Anna was also the President of Mexico, the Texans forced him to sign an agreement that recognized Texas as an independent nation. He and his men were forced to return to Mexico.

Mexico and the Newly Independent Texas, 1838
(*Source:https://www.raremaps.com/gallery/detail/37793/*
a-map-of-mexico-and-the-republic-of-texas
-1838-niles-pease)

The Republic of Texas and the Undefined Lands

With the war over, Texas and Mexico had to establish the terms for its end. The new Texas government stopped the land grant system that had dictated who controlled the lands of the new nation.

Soldiers were given time to find homes as they had been the ones to sacrifice the most for the Republic of Texas.

However, there was not an agreement between Mexico and the Republic of Texas as to what the new republic included. The Republic of Texas thought that it now had more than twice the lands that had made up the few territories that made up Texas before the war. As shown below, Mexico considered the vast majority of the lands still to be in their possession. Neither of the two nations officially settled the dispute over the lands, and this would come to be a source of much larger dispute within the next two decades as the US began to finally consider what to do about the Republic of Texas, which had been looking to join the country even before they were separate from Mexico.

Disputed Lands between Mexico, Texas, and the US
(*Source: https://upload.wikimedia.org/wikipedia/
commons/0/09/Republic_of_Texas_lab*

Chapter 8 – Annexation to the US and the Mexican-American War

As Texas and Mexico fought for control of the lands that truly belonged to the native peoples, the US watched with interest. Though they were unwilling to do anything that could upset the Mexican government, they were interested in seeing how the war would be resolved. They stood to gain more from an independent Texas, and that raised the question of whether they should annex the region.

There were several very important reasons the US was hesitant to annex Texas despite Stephen Austin's pleading to intervene on behalf of the settlers, who were once American. The fear of a war with Mexico was a major concern, but there was a much more divisive problem with incorporating Texas. It involved the already strained relationship between those who wanted to abolish slavery and those who wanted to perpetuate it. However, fear of a war with Mexico was the primary reason behind US reluctance to help.

The initial refusal of the US to incorporate Texas into the country was troubling for the Texans. Having alienated nearly every group around them, the Texans knew that it was only a matter of time before their neighbors would band together to snuff them out. The Cherokee had shown a willingness to work against the Mexicans prior to the revolution, but instead of fostering this relationship, which the newly elected President Houston advocated, Texas continued to try to pressure the US into annexation.

After a decade, the US finally decided that annexing Texas was not as much of a risk as it had been during the war. It would be a messy endeavor, but by the end of the 1840s, Texas would officially become the 28th US state. After the annexation, the US instigated a war with Mexico to settle a dispute about where the boundaries of Texas should be drawn. No longer afraid of war, the US started the Mexican-American War.

Texans' Long-standing Expectations Fulfilled

The first official move to join the US came in 1836 when the first elections were held after the Texas Revolution. The people voted in favor of Texas being annexed into the US, but the Texas government failed to complete a treaty with the US that would ratify their statehood. The US was also reluctant to annex lands that had so recently been a part of Mexico.

However, once Texas had succeeded in winning its independence, the US kept an eye on the new nation and weighed its options. With more Americans streaming into Texas, some in the government also felt a sense of duty to protect those citizens. Texas did not force any of the immigrants to renounce their citizenship, so the new settlers were largely American. American settlers continued to expect protection from the US, especially as tensions with the native tribes and the Mexicans mounted. There was ample evidence that Mexico was planning to initiate an attack, with some proof manifesting during the Cherokee War.

The Joint Resolution for Annexing Texas

Though it took nearly a decade, the US government finally reached a resolution that would allow Texas to officially enter the large nation as a state. Over the years, the US government had failed to agree to an official treaty with Texas, so they switched to another tactic to bring it into the union.

There were several reasons why it took so long to annex Texas. One of the most notable concerns for the US was the debt that Texas had incurred during their war for independence. The settlers had been prosperous under the Mexican government, but they were never wealthy, and the war resulted in a large debt that the US was not willing to take on. Another major issue was the rising division in the US about slavery. Each new territory that was brought into the country had to be assessed by abolitionists and the pro-slave lobbyists to determine whether slavery would be allowed in the future state. Adding Texas would mean giving the pro-slavery contingent a large swath of land, destabilizing the delicate balance among the existing states. Texans had already shown that they had no intention of giving up their slaves, even convincing the Mexican government to allow slavery in the territory prior to the revolution.

After the Texas Revolution, Mexico had made it clear that if the US annexed Texas, Mexico would take it as a declaration of war. For this reason, the US avoided any kind of negotiation until 1844. When the US started talking to Texas about the annexation, Mexico severed all diplomatic relations. US President John Tyler was unable to get the necessary votes in the Senate to ratify a treaty that had been negotiated with Texas that year. His next bid to annex the small nation was in 1845, a few months before he was to leave office.

When the US passed a joint resolution for annexation, it included three major conditions for the would-be state. First, Texas would remain in control of its public lands and its debts; the US would not manage them, which gave Texas considerable control over its own land. The second condition partly addressed the problem of slavery by leaving an option open for the US to decide that if it wanted to divide Texas into four new states, it would have the right to do so. Finally, the US government would be responsible for providing governmental facilities, postal services, and military forces, and they would retain authority over the state as they did in all states in the union. That meant that Texas could control the land, but in exchange, they had to abide by American laws, particularly in areas where the US government was providing basic services.

By taking on Texas as a state, the US was taking a large risk. They would be building a governmental system that would run and operate on a much larger network, which would be costly. The annexation proposal was presented in July 1845 to a group of elected officials at the Constitutional Convention held in Austin. There were several proposals to consider, including the joint resolution for annexation and a peace treaty with Mexico. The peace treaty would finally settle the fighting between Texas and Mexico, but it required Texas to remain its own nation. If Texas opted to be annexed to the US, hostilities would continue. The end vote was exactly what was expected—the representatives voted to do what the people of Texas had wanted since before the Texas Revolution: to be annexed into the US. The proposal was then put to the people in October that same year. They voted to join the US, and annexation became official when the Annexation Ordinance and a state constitution were completed.

Texas submitted their votes to the US, and they were sent to Congress, where the decision of the people of Texas was quickly accepted. Before the end of 1845, the joint resolution to admit Texas into statehood was put before President James Polk for his signature. After nearly a decade of waiting, Texas was finally a state. The transfer of control began soon after, with formal transference occurring in February of 1846.

Mexico's Growing Concern

Mexican officials had been concerned that they would lose territory to the US even before the Texas war for independence. Once Texas had won its independence from Mexico without the help of the US, Mexico's fears about what could happen next intensified. Between 1836 and 1845, Mexico did everything in its power to dissuade the US from annexing the land that had so recently belonged to it.

One of the biggest points of contention between Texas and Mexico was how much of the territory belonged to Texas and how much belonged to Mexico. The total region in question would have more than doubled Texas. On its own, Texas did not pose much of a threat when it came to forcing Mexico to relinquish territory. That would change, however, if the US were to annex it. Besides fighting for their new state, Americans under the newly elected President Polk were seeking to bring to fruition the idea of Manifest Destiny. The Louisiana Purchase had helped to make this closer to reality during Thomas Jefferson's presidency, but the US was now eyeing Mexican territory in an effort to fulfill what they thought was right and inevitable.

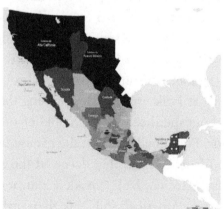

Mexico in 1845: In the Path of US Expansion
(*Source:https://en.wikipedia.org/wiki/Territorial_evolution_of_Mexic o#/media/File:Mapa_Mexico_1845.PNG*)

Initially, there was not much support on either side of the border for a war. However, Mexico was in a much weaker position: they were still attempting to build a nation amid civil wars and other power struggles. The US had been a nation for several decades and had coalesced around a strong central government. The odds were stacked against Mexico.

By annexing Texas, the US proved that it was finally willing to take over Mexican lands. After the annexation, the US began to claim ownership of lands that were still in dispute. Prior to gaining Texas, the US had sent John Slidell and a small contingent of politicians to Mexico to negotiate the purchase of a large swath of the northern area of Mexico. The US wanted to replicate the cheap cost of the Louisiana Purchase, which had more than doubled the size of the US in 1803 for fifteen million dollars (or eighteen dollars per square mile). Slidell was authorized to offer thirty million dollars for the region, but the Mexican government would not even meet with him, as they had no desire to sell the lands.

When Slidell returned saying that Mexico was unwilling to meet with him, President Polk decided to market it as an insult to the nation. Polk then forced a war with Mexico because he believed it was the only way to potentially acquire the lands he believed were destined to be a part of the United States. To ensure that the US military would instigate a war, he sent troops to reside in the disputed region south of the Texas border. These troops were technically invading another nation, and unsurprisingly, Mexico fired on them. This was exactly what Polk wanted. By spinning the invasion by the US into a story about the death of a US soldier on US lands at the hands of Mexicans, Polk finally created the excuse he needed to start a war to steal land from Mexico. He deceived the American people when he said that Mexico had "invaded our territory and shed American blood upon American soil." He then ordered Congress to declare war. Many Americans questioned this. Northern states said that Polk, who was a Southerner, was attempting to acquire more slave-holding states and give greater control to them. There were also many Americans who simply did not want to go to war to steal lands from another country, for it had been less than one hundred years since they had won their own freedom. Many people still felt strongly that the US should not be an aggressor (except when it came to displacing the Native Americans). Despite the protests of many Americans, Congress gave their approval on May 13th, 1846.

The Mexican-American War

The Mexican-American War would later be described by a young second lieutenant named Ulysses S. Grant as a war that was "one of the most unjust ever waged by a stronger against a weaker nation. It was an instance of a republic following the bad example of European monarchies, in not considering justice in their desire to acquire additional territory." This was exactly what had made many Americans oppose the idea of war before it was declared. However, once they were committed, many Americans felt it was necessary to provide support and boost the morale of the soldiers. Even if the war was wrong, the Americans did not blame the soldiers. The Mexicans, on the other hand, were not only against the war but also not in the position to benefit from it. America was now an aggressor that had largely been at peace since winning its independence, in stark contrast to the chaotic aftermath of the Mexican War of Independence. Mexican morale was already low, and this was yet another fight, but this time against a much more powerful force. The Mexican soldiers and people were as aware as Ulysses S. Grant of the superiority of the US forces.

Three notable officers fought in the Mexican-American War: General Zachary Taylor, Ulysses S. Grant, and Robert E. Lee. This was both Grant and Lee's first experience fighting in a war. Despite the novice US commanders and the superior numbers of the Mexicans, the Americans managed to quickly rule the battlefield.

The Mexican-American War began in April 1846 with 8,000 American soldiers. Wanting to provide support and fight for their country, more than 60,000 Americans soon joined as volunteers. There were over 73,000 Mexicans, who were also a mix of regular soldiers and volunteers. The Mexican Navy couldn't contend with the much more robust US Navy. But annexing Texas was not enough: Manifest Destiny had to be fulfilled. To further undermine Mexico, Polk sowed discontent in the other Mexican territories of modern-day California by sending John Fremont and Stephen Kearny to instigate a revolution in the area. Thus, the people in California declared themselves the Bear Flag Republic even before they learned of the fighting between Mexico and the US. Led by Fremont, they marched on a military outpost, a Mexican presidio, and secured the region for the US. While Fremont was ensuring the theft of the California territory, Kearny was enacting a similar strategy in New Mexico, driving the governor out of the region. He and his band captured the capital, and after their success, Kearny led his men west to join with the successful Californians.

As Kearny and Fremont secured the northern region, Generals Zachary Taylor and Winfield Scott marched on Mexico City. Taylor faced Antonio López de Santa Anna directly and headed toward the capital's center while Scott approached the city from a different direction. Scott and his men successfully took control of the city, leaving the Mexicans with no option but to surrender in September of 1847. This put the US in a better position to negotiate for land at a much lower cost.

Ironically, the annexation of Texas and the Mexican-American War would be two major contributing factors to the American Civil War. By pushing for something that most Americans did not want, the nation became even more bitterly divided. Discussions about Polk's underhanded methods and unconstitutional behavior in essentially forcing the country into an unjustified war became widespread. One of the nation's most notable writers of the time, Henry David Thoreau, believed so strongly that the war was wrong that he was arrested for refusing to pay taxes in protest of the war.

His protests begat *Civil Disobedience*, an essay that is still used today to enact peaceful change.

These events were all a prelude for what would come later. The acquisition of so much land by a nation that was already so divided would result in far more internal hostilities. By winning the Mexican-American War, the US all but assured that it would tear itself apart just a couple of decades later. The Missouri Compromise of 1850, which was meant to address the question of whether the new American lands would be slave states or free states, would ultimately be the undoing of the US for many years.

Treaty of Guadalupe Hidalgo

It is also ironic that the treaty to end the war was made without the president's knowledge. Signed on February 2nd, 1848, the treaty set the boundaries for the regions that would be a part of the US going forward, including all the southwestern states of the US today.

Lands Lost after the Mexican-American War
(*Source:https://en.wikipedia.org/wiki/Mexican_Cession#/media/File: Mexican_Cession.png*)

Mexico received nearly half the money that had been offered to them prior to the war, with all this land becoming a part of the US for between fifteen and eighteen million dollars (the US also took on some of the Mexican debt for these regions, increasing the total cost of the lands). The disputed lands with Texas (shown in the previous chapter) were identified, and new borders were drawn. A single war lost Mexico over half of its total land. Polk endorsed the treaty, then sent it to Congress for final approval. It passed by a vote of 34 to 14 in March 1848.

There was a sense of victory in the US following the completion of what it believed to be inevitable Manifest Destiny. However, the results of the war further widened the divide between abolitionists and slave owners. While it was inevitable that the slavery issue would need to be resolved, the addition of so much new territory and no ability to ensure that slavery did not spread into the territories where it was banned would force a struggle that soon became open warfare.

Chapter 9 – Role in the Civil War

Texas had finally achieved what many of the American settlers had expected on December 29, 1845. Had the settlers better understood the tensions in the US, they likely would have decided against seeking entry as a state. The US was moving in the same direction as Mexico: slavery was quickly becoming untenable to most Americans. While Texas fell firmly on the pro-slavery side, the South was significantly outnumbered by the North in terms of population.

The fears of US Congress members who had wanted to avoid annexing Texas because of the unbalance it would likely cause in the current unrest proved to be well-founded in 1861. Many Texans were much more inclined to find a peaceful resolution with the northern states than they had been with Mexico, but they were unwilling to compromise when it came to retaining their slaves. There were other concerns, such as the fear that northerners would force their views on southern states, but ultimately it was the fear of the slaveholders that drove Texas to join the other southern states in seceding from the nation they had joined less than two decades earlier. Though the primary battles occurred in the eastern states, Texas did have a significant role to play in the American Civil War.

The Election of Abraham Lincoln and the Texas Convention to Address Secession

Many of the southern states were unsettled by the election of Abraham Lincoln to the presidency. In November of 1860, Sam Houston was the Texas governor, and he had worked hard for the annexation of Texas. Despite his misgivings for the direction the US was taking, he was unwilling to do anything that would jeopardize the state's place in the country. As Texans called for their governor to hold a convention to discuss the state's next moves, Houston refused. He knew that they were going to discuss the possibility of secession, and he would not do anything to support such an action. When South Carolina seceded in December of 1860, other southern states were holding their own conventions to discuss following South Carolina's example.

A group of prominent Texans, including Oran M. Roberts, George M. Flournoy, and John S. Ford, formed a group to force the discussion. They wanted to hold a convention in the early part of January 1861. To thwart the convention, Houston called for a special legislative session that he hoped would reject any recognition of the convention. The session was held, but it did not go as Houston had hoped. Instead of refusing to acknowledge the convention, the legislature approved it with the stipulation that the people of Texas would get a final vote on its outcome.

The convention began on January 28, 1861, ironically meeting in Austin, Texas. Had Stephen Austin still been alive, he probably would have opposed the move, yet they were meeting in the capital city named after him to undo one of the last major fights he had engaged in—joining the US. Most of the people who attended the convention were in favor of secession, and the ordinance was adopted on February 1st. The final vote in favor of secession was 166 to 8, and it was approved. Following the successful passage of secession, the convention met again to make the final declaration that they were leaving the US to join the Confederate States of American.

Houston refused to acknowledge the decisions of the convention and would not take an oath to what he saw as the illegal and treasonous turning on the US. Consequently, Houston was deposed as Governor. They then filled the position with Edward Clark, the Lieutenant Governor.

Lincoln was sworn into office on March 4, 1861, and to support Houston's resistance to the secession, he told the legendary leader that he was willing to send troops to Texas. However, Houston's anger at the secession of Texas did not mean that he was willing to incite violence within the state. To reduce the violence and threat of a civil war within the state, Houston retired and moved to Huntsville, Texas. He did not live to see the end of the war, as he died in Huntsville in 1863, a year before the war ended.

Movement to Take Control of Federal Lands and Supplies

As the convention was preparing to take its next steps, the committee sent troops to remove the US army from Texas. The Confederate troops first went to confront Major General David E. Twiggs, who commanded the American troops in Texas. He quickly agreed to surrender and remove nearly 3,000 Union soldiers who were currently working around the state, including in the frontier. After the Union soldiers left, Confederate troops occupied the many shelters and fortifications around the frontiers of the state.

While Texas soldiers wanted to contribute to the war, Texans understood they could not simply abandon the frontiers. If their people were left unprotected, sentiment could easily shift against the elitists who focused on fighting the US instead of protecting their own citizens. Even though just over 46,000 Texans voted for secession, nearly 15,000 people had voted against it.

The state had a large German population who were very much against the move, and they formed what came to be known as the Union Loyalty League. Their presence, along with Texans who were loyal to the US, was sizeable enough that violence within the state required the government to declare martial law in regions with high loyalist populations. Others sought to leave Texas to live in the US, particularly those who were born in the north and had migrated to Texas following its annexation.

The Confederates were vicious in trying to put down any Union sentiment or loyalty. For example, they tried and executed the US loyalist Josefa "Chipita" Rodriguez, claiming with no supporting evidence that she had killed a traveler, John Savage. Union loyalists who tried to leave were often hunted down and killed.

When the year ended, 25,000 Texans had joined the fledgling Confederate States Army. An estimated two-thirds were cavalrymen, in large part because their experiences in the frontier made them adept horsemen.

The Drawn-out War

Initially, the Confederacy seemed to be doing very well against the Union. However, it was ultimately a war of attrition, with most of the battles occurring in southern states. The fervor that the southern states felt in the beginning helped to bolster several critical wins. Ultimately, the Confederacy had to win the war quickly to remain their own nation, though. The US army was not as familiar with the lands where the fighting occurred, which was another advantage to the Confederacy. As the war moved into a second and then a third year, it became obvious that the Union had all the critical advantages to conduct a longer war. They had a much larger population, which meant that troops were not pushed to the same limits as Confederate troops. The perpetual fighting hampered and then began to break the enthusiasm that had boosted the South in the beginning. The North also had a significant advantage in terms of resources. Most of the nation's manufacturing and resource production occurred in the North, while the South was predominantly agricultural. As many of the battles occurred in the South, food production was interrupted and crops destroyed, reducing even this resource for the southern army.

Texas was not affected nearly as much as the southeastern states because it was not as critical as states such as Virginia and Georgia to winning the war. If the most important states in the Confederacy could be brought down, Texas would have no recourse but to accept defeat. It would have been interesting to have seen what would have happened to Texas had they either not joined the US in 1845 or seceded to become their own nation instead of joining the rest of the South in the Confederacy. The US would not have been able to fight both the Confederacy and Texas, which would have given Texas four years to fortify themselves against war with the US. It is uncertain whether the US would have been willing to re-enter another war after four years of fighting against the Confederacy.

Since Texas did tie themselves to the Confederacy, they were not immune to attacks by Union soldiers. It is estimated that 70,000 to 90,000 Texans joined the Confederate Army over the years. At least thirty-seven Texans held prominent roles in the Confederate Army, as well. The only two major battles after Texas' secession that did not include Texans were First Manassas and Chancellorsville.

One population that had been growing since the Texas Revolution were Mexican Americans. Mexicans had joined the American settlers during that war, and many Mexicans fled the political upheaval and uncertainty of Mexico, choosing to live in Texas. They were often the targets of extreme racism, even by the law enforcement agency of Texas Rangers. With a large population of Mexican Americans not willing to leave the US to become a nation that was attempting to perpetuate institutional racism through slavery, there were soon significant fights between Texans and Mexican Americans. Both sides sought to recruit the large Mexican American demographic. Since many Americans had married Mexicans, the lines were not as well established, though, and about 2,550 Mexican Americans decided to help the Confederacy. However, nearly 1,000 joined the Union, a much higher percentage than any other demographic who were unhappy with the departure of Texas from the US.

Most Texas soldiers remained in Texas to fight Union soldiers trying to infiltrate Texas. One of the reasons why so many soldiers remained in Texas was that the Union was not the only enemy that Texans faced. Though their numbers had been significantly reduced, there were still many Native Americans who were taking advantage of the American Civil War to attack settlers on the frontier, most notably the Comanches. Mexicans were also turning the Civil War to their advantage, with many raiders attacking settlements and towns in the southern parts of the state.

Western Texas became a place of refuge for deserters from both sides of the war, outlaws, and settlers who sought protection after abandoning their homes because of Native American raids. This strange combination of different groups of people was a major reason Texas is associated with the Wild West. As there was little military presence in the western part of the state, these groups created their own set of laws (or failed to make any), and lawlessness was rampant. It was impossible for Texas to protect such a large area, so they chose to fight the Union to the north and east, and Mexicans to the south. The west was largely left to its own devices and became a region where many outlaws made their home.

Despite the lack of any real protection from the Texas military in the west, the Confederacy wanted to expand into the west, at least in the beginning of the war. Initially, the Confederacy succeeded, as the US did not have an adequate military presence in these territories. The Texans accomplished a measure of success as they pushed into the New Mexico territory, which was part of the Union. This victory was quickly stymied, then put down, as the US took control of the supply chains. The Union also mobilized soldiers located in California, resulting in the withdrawal of the Confederacy from the western regions they had claimed.

Another problem that Texas faced that the other southern states did not was a dearth of railroads. As a massive state that was still new to the US, there had not been adequate time to build the kinds of intricate railroad systems that were needed to supply the many different outposts. Having to rely on stagecoaches quickly proved problematic for the Texas Confederates, as the Union could easily interrupt and stop their supply chains. Keeping their ports open in the Gulf of Mexico was important, and, initially, Texas was successful there. Then the US sent superior and better-equipped ships to take control of the critical port in Galveston, Texas—the largest seaport in Texas—which they needed for the supplies that arrived from other Confederate states and nations. The Union managed to take control of the port in October 1862, but the Confederates recaptured it just after New Year's Day in 1863. Despite the Confederacy's success at reclaiming Galveston, the Union had established and maintained a blockade, which became more robust every month. Initially, the blockade did not appear to be very successful as ships slipped through several times a week. But, as the Union wore down the other southern states, they could focus more on the Gulf Coast to prevent supplies from moving freely.

Ironically, Texas ended up turning to Mexico for resources. With tensions still very high (it wasn't even twenty years since the revolution), Texans resorted to smuggling goods across the border, as Mexico had no reason to provide them with any substantial support. Still, Mexico was willing to trade for cotton, and it didn't hurt for Mexico to help both sides. After all, they had as much reason to loathe the US as Texas. Keeping the fight going could both provide them with extra resources and weaken their northern neighbors.

The longer the war dragged on, the more ordinary life changed in Texas, even in areas that were far from conflict with Mexico and Native Americans. Food production was increasingly rationed because such a large portion was required for the soldiers. Slaveholders also moved from other states into Texas, which saw a rise in the number of slaves from 182,000 to 230,000, largely because Texas was far less affected by the war than the other states. This put free African Americans in peril because slave owners did not respect the fact that they were free and would often force them into slavery. Many left the state as a result.

End of the War

Texas contributed many soldiers to fight the Union, but ultimately, the Confederacy could not win a long war. Their only real hope of winning was to win quickly. On April 9, 1865, General Robert E. Lee signed the Confederate surrender, and the next month saw the surrender of other Confederate departments.

As it became clear that the war was ending, Texas Governor Pendleton Murrah tried to ease the transition by issuing three different proclamations:

1. He ordered all Texas civil officers to keep control of all public property.

2. He requested a special legislative session.

3. He called for the election of new delegates for a new convention.

Unfortunately, his proclamations were too little, too late. Confederate soldiers had already begun to disband because they had not been paid for months, and it was clear that they weren't going to be paid. As they left, the soldiers took whatever they could. Chaos and disorder quickly spread, as soldiers started to follow their basic instincts to survive over all else.

This was not the biggest concern for men like Murrah, though. Those who had served in prominent positions in the Confederacy were facing serious charges and repercussions for treason as the war ended. Opting to flee instead of face the consequences, many of the most prominent people in Texas left the state to save themselves. This meant that there were far too few leaders in the state at a time when it desperately needed them. Following the assassination of President Lincoln in April of 1865, President Andrew Johnson was faced with having to help rebuild all the southern states while trying to establish himself as a leader. Johnson finally appointed a new government for the state of Texas in June, and he chose A. J. Hamilton, a former Texas congressman in the US legislature. Until Hamilton's arrival, a Union soldier, General Granger, oversaw Texas, and one of his first actions was to declare that Texas slaves were now free. Today, Texas still celebrates June 19th as Emancipation Day.

One of the first things that Governor Hamilton did was to call for all loyal men to join in a convention in Austin to discuss the future of the state. Based on what President Johnson had instructed, Hamilton was seeking to establish a new government as quickly as possible and restore the relationship between the state and federal government. Texas would not be allowed to govern itself for almost a decade.

Chapter 10 – Reconstruction

For the first time, the people of Texas lost their bid for something they wanted, showing just how much different being a part of the US was compared to being a part of Mexico. The US was older, better established, and even during the Civil War, they had established agreements with other nations that helped to push them forward. Now those same people were responsible for the future of the state. Texas had lost its heroes from the Texas Revolution, and those who had pushed them into seceding had fled. While Governor Hamilton had represented Texas in the US Congress, he could be considered disconnected from the state after four years of war.

Like the rest of the former Confederate states, Texas experienced a serious economic upheaval and shift in its workforce. Plantations and ranchers no longer had free labor, and there was fear of the resentment that may occur now that African Americans were free. People who had once held sway over the state found themselves with far less power. The state had to learn to evolve and navigate an uncertain future.

Arrival of US Forces

With the end of the war, the US began sending troops into southern states, which meant the recent enemies of Texas were controlling the state. The forces began to arrive in May 1865, making Texans very uncomfortable. Each of the commanders who entered the state had their own idea of what they were to do in Texas, though most of them believed their first job was to ensure the freedom of former slaves and make sure their rights weren't violated. There was also a strong sentiment that the people of Texas should remain under military control until they had proved they were once again loyal to the US. The commanders didn't agree on what would prove that people were loyal, which could have led to decades of military occupation. This would clearly not make the people feel like they were part of the country, but more like prisoners in the US. Fortunately, the US military could not spare numerous soldiers to any single state for long, so the fears that the military would interfere in the Texas economy would prove to be unfounded.

Initially, 51,000 soldiers were sent to Texas, but a year after the end of the war, that number diminished to 3,000. Just as before the war, many of those soldiers were stationed near the frontier to protect the people from the same threats they had been facing from the Native Americans and Mexican raiders. The military was unable to enact much change across the state because they simply did not have the number to enforce the laws.

The Founding of the Freedmen's Bureau and Expressed Interests by Former Slaves

Of greater concern to the old power structure in Texas was the creation of the Bureau of Refugees, Freedmen, and Abandoned Lands, better known as the Freedmen's Bureau. The Bureau was formed under the control of Major General Edgar M. Gregory. Beginning in September of 1865, the Bureau managed the oversight of any events or actions that pertained to freedmen, refugees, and lands that had been abandoned, usually by Confederate officials or representatives who fled. Its most time-consuming and important task was ensuring that the former slaves could transition into life as free men. Gregory quickly showed that he would take a much more conservative approach to how this should happen, making it easier for the older Texan families to feel comfortable with his actions. His approach was usually to force former slaves to return to the lands that they had previously worked and resume the same work they had once done. To keep them on these lands, the Bureau often forced former slaves to sign contracts that would require them to work there at a stipulated wage. It was almost impossible for former slaves to fight this since they had no way of acquiring lands on their own. Just as they had done when Mexico banned slaves, the plantation and ranch owners used debt servitude to make it all but impossible for most slaves to leave because they were not paid enough. Essentially, they would have to pay for the places where they had been forced to live as slaves, which would leave little to no money left of the wages that they earned.

Texans wound up pleased with the way Gregory ensured that laborers were plentiful and that there was minimal economic impact on the wealthy landowners. What he implemented that upset many white Texans was the effort to educate the former slaves. White Texans were further angered by what they considered interference in how their judicial systems treated African Americans. These criticisms were common, but the reality was likely far less impactful than the complaints implied. The US government did not have adequate funds to provide substantial education to the recently freed people, nor did it have enough personnel to significantly protect the freedmen. It is likely that the Texans were simply complaining because they believed that their power had been reduced, not about any noticeable changes. The people were more concerned with potential changes to the status quo than what was accomplished during the first couple of years.

The biggest threat came from the freedmen themselves. Having been given their freedom, former slaves wanted to have the same opportunities as their white counterparts. From pushing for education to wanting to control their own work schedule, freed slaves were pressing for rights to be guaranteed to all people in the US. This was the most obvious threat to the former slave owners, as well as those who had never had enough money to own slaves. The freedmen could work for less, or so it was thought, which meant that it would be harder for white people to find jobs. The freedmen wanting to control their schedules and living conditions was considered a burden to the people who used to own and control all aspects of their slaves' lives. White Texans began to openly oppose the push to improve the lives of former slaves, often resorting to threats or violence. In response, the freedmen demanded that the US provide legal protections against the offenders. They began a coordinated effort to petition for protection, meeting in Austin on March 10, 1866. The conference resulted in representatives demanding voting protections and that the state provide public lands for education. From this meeting, the Austin Freedman's Society formed, which would become the core of the African American Republican Party.

A False Start at Returning to the US as a State

President Johnson set the rules that would allow Confederate states to return to the US. All the states were put under the control of an appointed governor who would oversee the states' progress in meeting those requirements. The initial work for governors had three parts: governors ensured that the act of secession implemented in all southern states was nullified, initiated and enforced the abolishment of slavery, and repudiated the debt accrued by all the Confederate states.

For the most part, the way governors implemented the changes was intended to help restore the states' legislatures. Conventions were held, and the delegates who participated were required to take the oath of amnesty. Only voters who had also taken the oath could elect delegates. They then ratified the decisions that were passed by the delegates during the convention and would be allowed to elect their own governor, legislature, and officials. Once repopulated by representatives who had sworn to be loyal to the US, the state legislatures would have to ratify the 13th Amendment, which abolished slavery in the US.

With the arrival of Governor Hamilton, many of the Union supporters either returned to the state or found themselves in a position of control. This was one intention behind the requirements for restored statehood: the president was looking to prevent the old antebellum leaders from having any say in the direction their states would take. The president and other US leaders knew that allowing the antebellum leaders to continue to have a voice would not only jeopardize the return of the states into the Union but also prevent the full abolishment of slavery. Their exclusion from power ensured minimal issues in restoring the states to the US.

Hamilton was not as effective as some of the other appointed governors, and he was unable to prevent the previous leaders from gaining considerable power within Texas. The election of January 8, 1866, saw the state's old power dynamics largely resumed. This was possible because these leaders had not lost much of their economic control over the states and had hindered others from rising to power. When the Texas convention was held in February of 1866, many of the leaders were the same as those who had agreed to secession. Because of this, there were many more concessions made between the two sides. In the end, Texas did only the minimum to return to the US as a state. The convention quickly passed many of the laws enacted during the war that were not in direct violation of the US Constitution.

Forcing out the Antebellum Leaders

The problem with Texas' return to the US became clear when the Texas legislature refused to ratify either the 13th or 14th Amendments. To further insult the requirements, the legislature passed what were called "black codes" that dictated how freedmen could work within the state, giving most of the control to the antebellum leaders. The Unionists in the state quickly decided that the people in power were not only unrepentant for the war they had caused but also determined not to abide by the requirements to return to the country. Consequently, none of the elected officials were permitted to assume their roles in Washington, D.C. Nor was Texas the only state that proved it had learned almost nothing from the Civil War.

Because of the difficulties encountered during the first few years after the Civil War, the US Congress passed the First Reconstruction Act. This required the states that had seceded from the Union to be divided into different military districts controlled by the US military. Texas was a part of the Fifth Military District under this new law. Governor James Throckmorton was removed from office by General Griffin, who became manager of the district in March of 1867. Griffin died a few months later from the yellow fever epidemic and was succeeded by Joseph Reynolds. Reynolds pushed for the implementation of reforms Griffin had intended to make, including several special orders that removed many of the elected state officials from their positions—including over 400 county officials, the city officials who were elected in San Antonio, and most of the officials in Austin. Reynolds appointed people whom he trusted or who were known to be loyal to the US and had completed the Congress "Ironclad Test Oath," which required officials to swear that they had never taken up arms against the US. This excluded nearly all the antebellum leaders, ensuring they were not able to return to power. Considering the size of the state, it was nearly impossible for Reynolds to oversee all the positions, so he had others manage positions on the local level. Officials who could not pass the test would be considered incapable of holding their positions. As of April 25, 1869, all the positions held by unqualified personnel were considered vacant.

The First Reconstruction Act created further steps that all former Confederate states had to take before they would be able to send representatives to the US government. Another convention was held, and it was decided that the only individuals not able to become officials were women and felons. Any man who was at least twenty-one years old and had not been convicted of a felony could be a delegate, even a former slave. The convention would dictate that a new constitution be written for each former Confederate state, and each state would have to ratify the 13th and 14th Amendments. Only then would the US Congress consider readmission of that state into the Union.

Conservatives in Texas decided not to vote, hoping to deny a majority vote for what was to come. Because of their refusal to vote (even though many had registered), the radical Republicans easily carried a majority. The convention was held from June 1, 1868, to February 1869.

Whereas most former Confederate states had to contend with opportunists who used the devastation from the war to enrich themselves during reconstruction, Texas had a largely unique problem. Because of how expansive the state is, lawlessness was a significant problem except in the major cities and large towns. There were many outlaws who could easily escape the laws as the state tried to draft a new constitution. This would be a residual problem long after Texas was returned to the Union.

Chapter 11 – Texas Rangers – One of the Most Illustrious Law Enforcement Agencies

When Moses Morrison asked for volunteers to protect settlers, he could not have imagined how instrumental that group would become, eventually evolving into the law enforcement agency known as the Texas Rangers. From their humble beginnings, the Texas Rangers would go through many different changes, and not always for the better, eventually becoming one of the most well-known agencies in the US. Though not the oldest law enforcement agency (that distinction goes to the US Marshals Service), the Texas Rangers have become one of the most well-respected institutions, with their agents helping even other states to bring criminals to justice.

Original Role of the Rangers

The first Texas Rangers were not a part of any official organization. Volunteers who heeded the call in 1823, they doubled when Austin decided that more men were needed. With so many different people in the region, the original group of Rangers were as diverse as the populations who settled in Texas. There were frontiersmen who had learned how to live on the fringes of society, Native Americans who knew the region and wildlife, and a few members with considerable knowledge of guns. They were adept trackers, hunters, horse riders, and gunmen. They modified guns to make weapons that were ahead of their time. Yet these men largely worked for the greater good. Most of the time they worked well together, and their unique skills made the volunteer group one of the most effective protectors in Texas.

The Rangers would go on to fill similar roles over the years, protecting settlers during the War for Independence, as well as intimidating Mexicans who killed settlers. While their roles were largely as protectors instead of law enforcement officers for the first few decades, most of that would change once Texas became its own country.

Making Their Own Rules

With the new nation of Texas having little cohesion and few laws in place, the Texas Rangers started to operate by their own rules. Their primary role was to fight raiding Native Americans, but they soon lost sight of that, going against orders to drive Native Americans from their lands. They would also take a very aggressive approach against Mexicans, especially when they uncovered plots in which bandits sought to sow discontentment in the new nation.

Over time, the Rangers gained a reputation as protectors, and their aggression against other populations was welcome—largely seen as protective of the people. After Texas was annexed to the US, the Rangers would encounter fewer Mexicans trying to sow discord and had already successfully driven Native Americans from areas near settlements in most places.

Now there were fewer enemies, but the Rangers had come to expect a certain amount of respect and control wherever they went and soon began to use those aggressive tactics on Americans. It was only then that most of the people began to turn on the Rangers.

While the sentiment had been building near the end of the 19th century, by the early 20th century, most citizens had taken a much dimmer view of the Texas Rangers. For the next several decades, the group was viewed as a growing threat because of their cocky attitudes and lack of regard for the laws. Texans began to criticize them for resorting to violence before negotiating, a tactic that the Rangers had been using for decades without being questioned—until it was used against Texans.

It would take several more decades (roughly around the time of World War II) and a few highly reputable members to finally restore the Rangers to a place of honor and respect.

A Remarkable Record Against Notorious Criminals

Some of the loss of respect for the Rangers was unjustified, partly because they went after criminals who were considered heroes. One of the most notable criminals they captured was Sam Bass, a bandit who operated during the 1880s. The people loved him because he and his outlaws targeted the rich, and he often spent his money freely with the lower classes. Because of this, the people were angry when the Rangers finally caught up with Bass in July of 1887. During a shootout, he and his men managed to escape, but Bass had been shot by one of the Rangers. Bass would die the next day, July, 21st 1887, while in Ranger custody. This proved to the Texas legislature that the Rangers were still a formidable and necessary force. The Rangers initially gained the respect of the politicians, even if the people were unhappy with the way the Rangers had acted. Though Sam Bass was considered a hero, his band had not killed just the rich or those protecting their money: civilians had been killed, as well. The Rangers' use of force could be justified because Bass and his men would often shoot as soon as they knew law enforcement had found them.

The next infamous criminal that the Rangers tracked was John Wesley Hardin. They successfully captured him, but the legal system allowed this notorious criminal and murderer to be released under the guise of being rehabilitated. He then became a lawyer who hired others to kill for him. The Rangers did not track him again, largely because Hardin got sloppy after "going straight." When he failed to pay one of his assassins, the assassin killed him in a bar. The Rangers had not killed him, but they had done everything in their power to control this dangerous criminal who did not have the support of the people.

The most well-known criminals that the Rangers took down were Bonnie Elizabeth Parker and Clyde Champion Barrow, better known today as Bonnie and Clyde. Like Bass, they were criminals who were heroes to the people. Bonnie and Clyde did not help the people, but they operated during the Great Depression. Their ability to take from the rich to improve their own situation was admired by those who had no way to make a living. When they were ambushed and killed on May 23, 1934, their deaths were met with a mix of sadness and interest. They may not have helped the people, but they had done something to improve their own lot. Some civilians were killed because of them, which was partly why they were not mourned the same way Bass was mourned. Their notoriety is more closely aligned today with that of serial killers: their actions are considered wrong and immoral, but people cannot help but be fascinated by them.

These are some of the most notable cases the Rangers helped resolve, proving they had evolved into a law-abiding agency that could get difficult jobs done. Today they are a highly respected agency at the forefront of law enforcement agencies in the US. They help other agencies around the country resolve cases and review cold cases as new technologies evolve. One of the most notable cases they helped resolve recently was the murder of Irene Garza in April 1960. Though it took over 50 years, the Rangers were finally able to prove that she was murdered by a retired priest in 2016. Based on the evidence submitted by the Rangers and other members of law enforcement, Father John Feit was convicted of her murder and given a life sentence. This likely would not have been possible without the Rangers' dedication and constant review of the evidence and forensic techniques to finally see that justice was done.

Chapter 12 – Texas Tea – The Texas Oil Boom

As the state recovered from the economic devastation of the Civil War, a discovery was made that drew thousands of people in a hunt for riches. The state was not rich in gold, but by the end of the 19th century, there was a resource that had come to be more valuable to Americans than gold: Texas was rich in oil. The discovery in the small town of Corsicana would quickly transform it into a major industrial center. While oil had been found in Nacogdoches County back in 1866, the finding in Corsicana would begin to change the economy of the entire state.

An Accidental Find

When the American Well and Prospecting Company began drilling in Corsicana, they were interested in finding water. Instead of hitting water on June 9, 1894, they struck oil. The Corsicana City Council, which had hired them, paid only half of the agreed-upon fee because the company had not found the water they needed.

The initial production filled two and a half barrels a day, which was enough to attract plenty of attention to the region. Oil prospectors began drilling for other wells, hoping to find the rich deposits suggested by the initial find. The second well ended up being dry, but the next one, drilled in May 1896, provided a much higher yield than the first, filling over twenty barrels every day. About six months later, forty-seven wells had been drilled, and they produced nearly 66,000 barrels a day. To better handle the unexpected amount of oil, the first Texas oil refinery was built in 1897. This significantly increased how much oil could be pulled from the land, and 287 wells ensured that the refinery remained busy over the next few decades.

The American Well Prospecting Company began to focus on drilling oil, making its owners rich off both the oil they were putting into barrels and the technology they devised to better drill for oil. Seeing others come to the town with the hopes of finding oil, the company created a complementary business that repaired the devices used to pump oil. The company profited from the oil production and their unique understanding of how to drill for it (knowledge that was not as widespread since the only other place where oil and gas were mined with such fervor was in Pennsylvania). The company also developed the hydraulic rotary drilling rig and secured rights to the invention in 1900. This would be the rig that was used for a much larger oil discovery in 1901.

With the discovery of oil, Corsicana experienced a boom and an influx of financial wealth. The town had a new courthouse built in 1905, and its chamber of commerce was established in 1917.

The Lucas Gusher

The first major oil find was in Corsicana, but it was Spindletop that would cause the largest oil boom in Texas. On January 10, 1901, the mining engineer Captain A. F. Lucas was drilling in Spindletop when the ground shook, followed by an eruption from the drill site. Oil gushed up into the air like an exploding volcano, but with black liquid instead of lava. It was impossible to stop this outpouring, and thousands of barrels were released into the air and poured over the ground before the engineers were finally able to stem the flow. This dramatic eruption attracted a lot of attention from across the country, convincing many that there was a real chance of becoming rich by drilling in Texas. The event has often been replayed in movies and TV because of the incredible visual effect.

The Lucas Gusher significantly increased how much oil Texas produced, bringing the total number of barrels produced a year from just under 840,000 to nearly 4.4 million barrels by the end of 1901. Over the course of 1902, the small region of Spindletop saw the production of over 17.4 million barrels, which was over 94% of the oil produced in Texas that year. It also dropped the cost for a barrel of oil to just $0.03 per barrel.

A Second and Third Find in Corsicana

As drilling continued for the next fifteen years, the oil craze eventually began to settle down since, based on the amount of oil in the region, it seemed like production had stabilized. Then another deposit was found in 1923, and it caused a frenzy. During this time, known as the Roaring 20s, most of America was feeling positive about the economy, and many people were prospering. Seeing an opportunity to further improve their financial situations, people flocked to Texas in the thousands hoping to strike it rich. The fervor and drive resembled the handful of historic gold rushes that had caused people to uproot their families and stream west, but a much larger investment was required to drill for oil than to pan for gold.

Corsicana had once had an economy that was based on agriculture and shipping, but with each boom, the town changed. Following the first major oil boom, the town expanded far beyond any expectation. By the end of the second boom, it had become an industrial center and hub of oil production in the US. Many businesses grew up around the flocks of people who sought riches, largely to their detriment, as individuals could not reach the biggest deposits.

Due to the two major oil booms, Corsicana had become the wealthiest town in Texas. According to one reporter in 1956, more than twenty millionaires resided in Corsicana, with most of them making their fortune through the oil deposits, whether directly or indirectly (whether making repairs, selling goods, or building in the area). Later that year, a third deposit was found, and an additional 500 wells were drilled around Corsicana. There were so many drills and wells that one person described the sight of Corsicana as there being a drill in almost every person's backyard. By the end of the 1950s, more than 125 million barrels of oil had been collected in Corsicana.

The events over the span of sixty years significantly changed the history and economy of not only Corsicana but all of Texas. Without the first discovery of oil in the town, the rig used for the Lucas Gusher would likely have been less efficient, resulting in a much less dramatic finding.

The people of Corsicana continue to celebrate their good fortune every year at the Derrick Days Festival.

Timing Was Everything

One of the reasons that Texas gained so much attention for its oil deposits was the timing. The Native Americans had known about oil centuries before any of the Europeans arrived and had used it for medicinal purposes (though it is not entirely clear how they used it). The Spanish explorers had various uses for it, but primarily as a way of caulking leaks in their vessels. Until the 19th century, oil was not used as a primary transportation fuel. The combustion engine was first invented toward the end of the 18th century, but people did not realize its full potential until nearly 100 years later, with the advent of the first motor vehicles to use one. By 1886, motor vehicles were being produced with internal combustion engines, and the potential for oil to change the world began to increase the demand for the substance.

Because motor vehicles were not yet something that many people owned, the potential for this use of the oil was not recognized by the people of Texas who had hired well drillers. However, the American Well Prospecting Company that struck oil was very forward-thinking for the time and knew they stood to make a considerable profit from what they had found. Had they struck oil a few decades earlier, the finding would have been ignored, just like the first people who struck oil in Nacogdoches County. Ultimately, it was the timing of the find that would change the trajectory of drilling in the state.

Drilling would begin to occur in many places across Texas. Some of it was focused on finding water, but many people were hoping to strike oil. Offshore drilling began during 1908 near the island of Galveston, in the Galveston Bay. Initially, the drilling was unsuccessful, and many people gave up, leaving the field abandoned. In 1916, a gusher was found in the region, and many people moved there hoping that it was as rich in oil as Spindletop and Corsicana. When the people who managed W. T. Waggoner Ranch tried to drill for water on their lands in Wichita County in 1911, they encounter oil. This was one of four oil fields that would be established in the region. Oil was soon discovered at the Ranger Field in 1917 and Burkburnett townsite in 1918. The Texas oil boom was in full swing by the beginning of the Roaring 20s, and because of the changes in technology, the substance became incredibly valuable.

The biggest oil discoveries were in the eastern part of the state, in what is called the East Texas Oil Field. The oil in the region was found in October of 1930 by C. M. Joiner. The discovery was entirely unexpected, as the fields had already been condemned by geologists hired by major companies to find oil. Because of the find, many people began to fight for the right to lease land there. Considering the growing interest in the area, Texas Governor Ross Sterling requested the National Guard be deployed to the field to maintain order.

The finds were not all positive, though. Many people spent more than they could afford in hopes of finding oil, only to go bankrupt. There were many individuals and businesses who saw the oil fervor as a way to swindle those who didn't know much about drilling for oil. This extended to the stock markets, as the price per barrel was destabilized by new findings.

Today there are oil production facilities in over fifteen American states, but Texas is the best known for this industry because of the amount of oil it has produced. Texas continues to rely heavily on oil production for its economy.

Chapter 13 – The Space Race

One of the most quoted lines to come from Texas is the phrase "Houston, we have a problem." These words were uttered by an American astronaut who was radioing back to headquarters to try to get help in resolving a critical problem during a pivotal trip to the moon.

Houston has become one of the primary locations for the US National Aeronautics and Space Administration, or NASA. The agency was formed in response to the Soviet Union's launch of *Sputnik I*, which was the first artificial satellite to successfully reach Earth's atmosphere and orbit around the globe. The Soviet Union accomplished the successful launch of its satellite on October 4, 1957, and the US responded by passing the Space Act on July 8, 1958, and forming NASA. This was the beginning of the Space Race. Texas became instrumental in the US's efforts to achieve dominance in space.

The Formation of NASA and Its Rapid Advances

In response to the Soviet Union's satellite, the US formed NASA using existing governmental agencies, including California's Jet

Propulsion Laboratory. Eisenhower and his administration feared that the Soviet Union was pulling ahead in terms of technological advances and felt it was necessary to surpass the early Soviet accomplishments. The agency came together in October of 1958 with its primary objective to successfully launch a man into space, then return him unharmed. With its head start, the Soviet Union achieved this first when cosmonaut Yuri Gagarin reached Earth's orbit in April of 1961. The US was not far behind, though, as Alan Shepard became the first astronaut to reach space in May of 1961. He remained in the upper atmosphere for fifteen minutes. Less than a year later, in February 1962, John Glenn was the first American to enter Earth's orbit (the same feat as Gagarin).

Seeing that the Soviet Union was still about a year ahead in their technology, President John F. Kennedy announced to the US that he was initiating the Apollo Program, with the end goal of having a man walk on the moon and return unharmed.

Houston Becomes the Focus of the US Efforts in the Space Race

Before Kennedy's announcement, the beginning of the Apollo program was already underway. Knowing that they needed a dedicated facility, administrator James E. Webb began the hunt for a location to build a specialized facility, establishing the criteria that were necessary for success. The following were considered among the most vital needs for the new facilities:

1. The availability of both water transport and an advanced all-weather airport

2. A major telecommunications network near the facility

3. A large pool of potential support, including a well-established industrial economy and contractor support

4. A mild climate so that work could be conducted year-round

Houston met all these conditions and had the San Jacinto Ordnance Depot nearby. This depot offered additional benefits. For example, its military personnel had many of the important security clearances required for the NASA personnel already taken care of, and the supplies were more closely aligned with what they would need (compared to an established commercial block). There were also three prominent US universities nearby, including Rice and Texas A&M. By the end of 1962, construction on the facility was already underway. Among the first completed components were the simulations and operations so that astronauts could begin training for an experience that was largely guesswork up to that point.

The mission control center was built in Houston and has served as the major operational hub for all American space missions since Gemini IV that have required human pilots.

The Apollo Missions

Unmanned missions began in February of 1966, but the launch of humans into space had to be postponed because of the tragic accident that killed three astronauts in January 1967 as they rehearsed for the launch. Changes to the program were finally in place by October of 1968, and a new crew was selected. First, several Houston-controlled launches were conducted without any onboard pilots. Apollo 7 to 10 were all unmanned, as NASA tested and experimented with equipment.

The crew was finally launched with the goal of reaching the moon in July of 1969. Apollo 11 was on the way to deliver the first win to the US in the Space Race. On July 20th, the lunar module reached the moon, and Neil Armstrong because the first person to walk on its surface. Edwin (Buzz)Aldrin followed him a few minutes later.

The famous call to Houston occurred during the Apollo 13 mission in April of 1970. One of the oxygen tanks on the craft had exploded, damaging the craft and making it too risky for the astronauts to land on the moon. John L. (Jack) Swigert, the pilot for the command module, radioed back to the control center, saying, "Houston. We've had a problem here," which is slightly different than what is commonly quoted. He then went on to explain the problem, and against the odds, the engineers back in Houston were able to help the astronauts complete enough repairs to return to Earth. A movie based on the events was released in 1995, portraying a fraction of what the men experienced as they wondered if they would successfully return to Earth.

There were several more successful Apollo missions, up to Apollo 17. Most of them were exploratory missions in which astronauts brought back rocks and dust for further studies. The missions conducted a wide range of experiments on the moon, even hitting golf balls on the surface and driving specially-designed dune buggies. To better understand the atmosphere and environment of the moon, many of the Apollo missions conducted both solar wind experiments to see how humans would be affected and seismography measurements to determine how much of the surface could be used.

Apollo 17 was the final mission of the program, and it was completed in December of 1972. Between Apollo 11 and Apollo 17, a dozen Americans moved around on the moon, studying what was possible so far from home. Six of the missions were a success, with only Apollo 13 a failure because of the accident. The final walk on the moon occurred on December 14, 1972. The US has not sent any more astronauts to explore the moon, and no other nation has managed to achieve this singular experience.

Chapter 14 – Assassination of JFK

Although there have been many incredible events in Texas, one of the most notable in recent history was an incident that changed American history—the assassination of the 35th American President, John F. Kennedy (JFK). It has been nearly sixty years since November 22, 1963, yet the effects and legacy of that day are still ingrained in the memory of many Americans. It has also become one of the most controversial events in history, with numerous conspiracy theories formulated to explain what happened on that day in Dallas, Texas.

Preparing to Run for Re-election

As the end of 1963 neared, President John F. Kennedy was beginning to think about re-election and was in the process of starting up his campaign. His vice president was Lyndon B. Johnson, a man from Texas. During the 1960s, Texas was always politically unpredictable: they could vote for either a Democrat or a Republican for president. Knowing that Texas was a key state, it was important for Kennedy to spend some time there to persuade Texans he was still the right choice for the presidency. Though he had not yet declared that he was running for the office of president again, it was assumed that he would, and he wanted to act.

During the trip, Kennedy and his entourage traveled to nine states over the course of a week, including Texas. Ostensibly, the point of the trip was to highlight the government's efforts in managing natural resources and their conservation efforts. The real purpose, though, was to promote Kennedy as a president who focused on education, national security, and world peace. After all, he had helped to prevent a nuclear war during the Cuban Missile Crisis.

About a month after his trip around the country, Kennedy began to more openly campaign, taking a strategic approach by going to Boston and Philadelphia. He began to prepare for a lengthier strategy on November 12, 1963, and the two states that he felt were the most critical were Texas and Florida. To sway the voters, he planned to visit each state by the end of the month. The next stop on his path was Dallas, Texas. To prove that he was a family man, his wife was to accompany him to Texas. Mrs. Jacqueline Kennedy had been out of the public eye for several months after she and her husband had lost a baby in August. This was to be her first return to the campaign trail, and it was meant to be a chance to help her while supporting his political ambitions.

His presence in Texas was also meant to provide some unity within the Democratic Party, as the leaders of the party in Texas were split. In October, the United Nations Ambassador Adlai Stevenson was attacked in Dallas, so Kennedy felt his presence was needed to help calm the people of Texas, particularly in Dallas. Johnson visited just before Kennedy, essentially warming up the people of his state for the arrival of the president. Their first stop was in San Antonio, and then Houston. The president and his entourage then dined in Fort Worth with Congressman Albert Thomas to boost Thomas in the state.

November 22 and 24, 1963

The Kennedys woke in a hotel in Fort Worth. There was a steady drizzle of rain outside that did not dissuade a crowd of thousands from forming in the parking lot to see the first family. Kennedy ascended a platform and addressed the people. He talked about how strong the US was and how they were the first country in both defense and space exploration, with a strong economy that benefited the many. During this address, he had no kind of protection either from the light rain or interactions with the people.

Once his speech was over, he greeted people before heading inside for breakfast and gave another speech to the Fort Worth Chamber of Commerce. After breakfast, the procession headed to Carswell Air Force Base for a short flight to Dallas.

Upon their arrival in Dallas, both the president and the first lady addressed the people who were waiting at the fence along the exterior of the airport. They greeted individuals and thanked the people for coming out to see them. One of the well-wishers gave Mrs. Kennedy a bouquet of roses before the first family headed to meet with Governor John Connally and his wife for the trip into Dallas. The first family took the backseat in the convertible. The vice president and his wife were in a separate car in the motorcade.

After everyone was situated and ready to go, they began the ten-mile procession that went through the main streets of Dallas. The end destination was a shop where the president was to address a group of people at a luncheon. The procession slowly made its way down the streets lined with people excited to see the president and his wife. At 12:30 p.m., their car left Main Street near the Dealey Plaza and passed the Texas School Book Depository. As the procession passed the building, the sound of gunshots rang out in the air.

It is thought that three bullets were initially fired. One struck the president in the neck, and the next struck his head. The third hit the Texas governor in the back. The driver immediately sped up, heading to the Parkland Memorial Hospital that was only a few minutes from their position. Kennedy probably died as soon as he was struck by the second bullet. He was pronounced dead on arrival at the hospital, and a priest was brought in to give the nation's first Catholic president the last rites. The governor survived and eventually made a full recovery.

The president's body was loaded onto Air Force One to be taken back to Washington, DC, and on the trip, Vice President Johnson was sworn into office as president. President Kennedy was declared dead at 1 p.m. on November 22, 1963; President Johnson assumed the top position in the country at 2:38 p.m.

Lee Harvey Oswald was apprehended within two hours of the president's assassination. Two days later, on November 24, as Oswald was being transferred to the county jail, cameras were rolling as the news covered the story of the man who had killed a president. Suddenly, Jack Ruby stepped into the frame and shot Oswald in the stomach on live TV. Oswald died a few hours later at Parkland Hospital.

Aftermath

Kennedy was laid in state in the Capitol rotunda for twenty-one hours so that people could give their final farewells. An estimated 250,000 people visited during that time. Kennedy's son's farewell salute of his father's casket as it was taken to St. Matthews Cathedral was captured on film. The president was finally buried in Arlington National Cemetery a day after Oswald's death. Leaders and representatives from over 100 different countries paid their respects during the funeral.

By the end of November, President Johnson had appointed someone to investigate Kennedy's death and determine how it was possible that a president could be so easily killed. The appointee, Chief Justice Earl Warren, formed what came to be known as the Warren Commission, which was tasked with investigating the assassination of both the president and his assassin, Oswald. The commission issued its findings less than a year after the events of 1963, concluding that Oswald had acted alone. It further identified Jack Ruby as another individual who acted alone, killing Oswald out of a sense of vengeance. While less than 30% of Americans believed that Oswald had acted alone prior to the report's issuance, after the report, 87% of Americans believed there was only one assassin. This sentiment did not last long, and by 1966, people were already beginning to doubt the apparently rushed findings of the Warren Commission.

In response to rumors that the initial investigation had not had the full cooperation of all the federal agencies that were questioned, another committee was appointed to investigate the assassination in 1976. One of the findings from this second committee formed by the US House of Representatives was that there was almost certainly a second gunman—they did not think that Oswald had acted alone. This conclusion was based on a transmission tape that they had retrieved from Dallas that included evidence of at least four shots, perhaps more. This generated a lot of attention, and acoustic experts were called in to verify the sounds to see if the finding was accurate. According to the experts, the recording was too degraded to determine how many shots were fired; the tape was worthless. The same committee also investigated the assassination of Dr. Martin Luther King, Jr.

The Kennedy assassination not only revealed problems in how easy it was to gain access to the president but also put a spotlight on Texas and its response to the tragedy. While a lot of attention went to the Warren Commission, both the Texas attorney general and the Department of Public Safety initiated their own investigations into the events leading up to the assassination. Texas could be criticized not only for failing to protect the president but also for failing to secure the safety of the assassin.

A Wealth of Conspiracies

The assassination of John F. Kennedy has drawn a lot of attention, becoming a popular source for conspiracy theories. These theories only worsened following the re-opening of the investigation and the declaration that there was more than one assassin present that day, even after auditory experts discredited the tape. People have pointed to a wide range of evidence, such as scrapes in the concrete that were said to have hurt one of the people watching the procession, something that would not have been possible for Oswald to do. The initial disbelief that a single person could kill the president continues, and there is plenty of criticism of both the way local Texas officials and federal agencies had left many gaps in security. Americans have been coming up with many different explanations for what happened that day in 1963, from conspiracies claiming that the US government killed him, to speculation that the vice president was behind it (Kennedy was killed in Johnson's home state), to theories about aliens. It has become a favorite popular reference for TV, movies, and stories because of the amount of uncertainty that surrounds exactly what happened that day.

Chapter 15 – Texas Today

With its rich and varied history, Texas has evolved into a completely unique state within the US. It attracts millions of tourists every year seeking to learn the history of Texas, experience the Wild West in a much safer environment, and explore lands that were traveled by some of the most notable names in history.

Basic Texas Statistics

From a small group of settlements and large regions of indigenous people to the 28th state in the US to the center of the American effort in the Space Race, the evolution of Texas has made for some very singular statistics and a very diverse population. There are nearly 1,000 miles (1,600 km) between the northern and southern tip of the state and roughly the same distance between the east and the furthermost western side. Most of the state's boundaries are currently defined by bodies of water, including the Gulf of Mexico to the southeast and rivers that divide Texas from Oklahoma, Louisiana, and Arkansas. The Rio Grande is a large and beautiful border that divides a large portion of Texas and Mexico.

The state capital is still Austin, named for the first American to successfully establish an American settlement in the state. Today, Stephen Austin is known as the Father of Texas. Houston has the largest population in the state, and other major cities include Dallas, Fort Worth, and San Antonio. Dallas, Houston, and San Antonio all rank in the ten most populated cities in the US.

With the state becoming a hub for NASA, other technological industries have established footholds there, as well. The employment these industries represent has drawn a steady influx of people to Texas, and it is often one of the states with the largest population growth in the country. Starting in the 1970s, these trends have helped to change the state's demographics.

Texas's Evolving Economy and Education

Initially, Texas settlers prospered from farming and ranching. Following reconstruction, the state's economy became much more diverse, in large part because the Union began to try to modernize the south. Had the South had many of the economic benefits they gained after the war, they would have had a better chance of success. Before the Civil War, southern states primarily relied on slavery to prosper, as their economies were all based on farming and ranching. However, the economies did not entirely change; rather, the states expanded as they tried to learn how to work without slaves to support them. Cattle, cotton, and oil are all still primary sources of revenue for Texas, but the state has seen understandable growth in technology, banking, insurance, and construction as it has prospered over the last century.

There are over 140 colleges and universities in Texas, including community and junior colleges. The University of Texas, located in Austin, has about 50,000 students a year. Both the University of Texas and Texas A&M University have internationally-recognized graduate programs that attract people from around the globe every year. The prestigious private Rice University, located in Houston, produces graduates that meet higher than average academic standards.

Terrain and Climates

Texas can be divided into seven primary regions: Panhandle Plains, Big Bend, Hill Country, Prairies & Lakes, Piney Woods, South Texas Plains, and the Gulf Coast.

Coupled with its history, the diverse climate of Texas makes it an ideal place for visitors.

Texas Drought

While most people think of Texas as an expansive desert, it has a rich history of ranches and farming. During the early part of the 21st century, the state experienced serious droughts that are forcing ranchers to request assistance and look for innovative ways to take care of their cattle. Twenty-five percent of the population live in drought areas, with another 21% in abnormally dry areas. The southern regions of the state are the most adversely affected, and as late as 2020, there were many sites dedicated to monitoring the weather and temperatures to provide as much notification to ranchers as possible.

Conclusion

While all the states in the US have their own stories and histories, there is no history quite as singular as that of Texas. There is a reason why it is known as the "Lone Star State."

It is the only state that was once its own country and only became a country because the US would not annex it (Hawaii was its own country before US businessmen overthrew the Hawaiian monarchy, but up to that point, no nation claimed Hawaii as its own). Though most people are aware of the state's history as a stand-alone country, many are unaware of the time before this, and even less is known about the period before the arrival of Spain in the Western Hemisphere.

Texas is one of the few states that has seen an interesting mix of different demographics because of its pivotal role in the European exploration of North America. Initially, it was of little interest to the Spanish explorers as they learned that North America did not have the riches that they had found in South and Central America. Missionaries went out to try to convert the native peoples, and soldiers joined them to establish settlements, but that did not last long. France posed a threat to the Spanish claim, which was what drove the Spaniards to try to establish settlements. However, the Spanish were not accustomed to creating settlements from scratch, and this reduced their odds of success. As the territory became increasingly less stable and profitable, Spain began to look for ways to get more money from the region, even as they tried to control the growing resentment against them in Mexico City and around the colony. As Spain invited Americans to move to the region of Tejas, Mexico was waging a war for its own independence. By the time the first American settlers were ready to make the move to Texas, Spain was no longer in control of Mexico.

Mexico decided to continue the attempt to turn the northern regions into profitable settlements, so they made agreements like the ones that Spain had made with the Americans. The conditions were similar, but Mexico could not do much to ensure the settlers lived up to their end of the agreement. Relying on the leaders of the settlements resulted in growing resentment when Mexico tried to force the settlers to honor the agreements they had made. The fact that Mexico was slow to find its feet and civil war within Mexico quickly followed the end of the War for Mexican Independence revealed a weakness. When the settlers saw it, they started the War for Texas Independence, with the hope that the US would provide support and annex them into the country.

The Texans won their independence, but the US was hesitant to annex the small nation, knowing that the Mexicans would view it negatively. That sentiment changed about ten years later when the US president decided he wanted to realize the growing belief in Manifest Destiny. After the Mexican-American War, the desire for statehood was finally realized, but Texas would quickly learn that it should have remained its own country.

About fifteen years after becoming the 28th state, Texas joined the Confederates in seceding from the US. The Civil War and Reconstruction proved to be particularly trying times in Texas history, but with the help of the US government, the state was put on a path that would eventually lead to a much more diverse economy, with industries other than plantations and ranching. The state began to play a significant role in the US during the 20th century. From the establishment of the NASA main control center in Houston to the assassination of President Kennedy, Texas has continued to have a history that is completely unique.

Part 2: The Texas Rangers

A Captivating Guide to the History of a Law Enforcement Agency That Has Helped Stop Some of America's Most Infamous Criminals and Their Role in the Mexican-American War

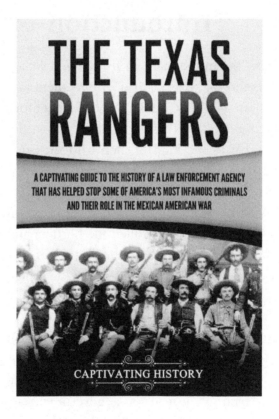

Introduction

Before Texas became a state in the United States of America, what would become the first state law enforcement agency would be formed. For about 150 years, this group of law enforcement agents has been viewed as both heroes and villains. Often portrayed in the movies and on TV as the kind of men who stick up for justice or who are the victims of truly sinister bad guys, the reality was far less black and white.

Founded by Stephen F. Austin in 1823, the Texas Rangers began as a group of volunteers who patrolled the borders and towns in the Mexican territory. Serving as both protectors of the settlers and police against criminals within the settlement, the Rangers had a wide range of skills. When they first started, they were simply ten men, but it grew quickly as more men volunteered. Over time, the number of American settlers who moved into Texas would outnumber the number of Mexicans. Following some changes in the way Mexico would govern states and settlements, Texans decided that they were living under a tyranny instead of a government like they were accustomed to in the US. With closer ties to the US than Mexico, Americans living in Texas would eventually decide that they needed independence from Mexico, starting the Texas Revolution in 1835.

By the end of it, Texas was an independent nation. It would be a few years before they would decide to become a part of the US, though.

While the Texas Rangers would turn on the Mexicans, it was the Native Americans that they would treat with utter contempt and cruelty from nearly the beginning. In the early days, some native peoples did join the Rangers, but after Texas split from Mexico, the hostile attitude adopted toward the natives made it nearly impossible for any of the Native Americans to continue to volunteer. Driving the people from their lands so that other Texans could take control of them, the Rangers were effective and ruthless. Some of this they had been able to master during the war, particularly the guerilla tactics they used. A six-month campaign joining the Tonkawas to remove the Comanches (a long-time enemy of the Tonkawas) would prove to be what launched the Rangers to the forefront of the Texas consciousness as being a more reliable source of protection. They would increasingly turn to the Rangers, who were less regulated than other armed forces, over the US military to protect them from perceived threats. As a result of this reliance on the Rangers, the members of the organization would become far more ruthless and aggressive in their approach to dealing with anyone they perceived as criminals.

In 1874, the Rangers became an official arm of the law based on legislation passed in Texas. One of their first official acts was to drive both the Comanche and Kiowa people out of Texas. This made potential settlers feel that Texas could be the ideal place to settle, as the Texas Rangers had proven their ability to drive away natives. The Rangers would further make new settlers feel safe as they kept the peace. However, the methods used to keep that peace were often questionable, and over time, the people of Texas became less eager to call on the Rangers. Over the years, the Rangers would be viewed as both heroes and villains, depending on who was leading the law enforcement agency and what methods the agency used to accomplish their goals. Sometimes fulfilling their roles earned them scorn, particularly when they captured or killed anti-heroes who were well-loved by the people. Other times, the Texas Rangers earned scorn through their cruelty and eagerness to resort to violence. Like much of the rest of the Wild West, the Texas Rangers have an interesting dichotomy that has earned them a famous and infamous place in American history.

One of the reasons that many people have heard of the Texas Rangers today (and why they are a popular choice for TV and movie characters) is because of the role they have played as law enforcement agents. They are nearly as well known as the FBI and are better known than nearly any other law enforcement agency. Over more than one hundred years after its formation, they would be responsible for taking down some of the most infamous Americans, including the romanticized Bonnie and Clyde.

Their role in US history is both solid and liquid; they have been an ever-present force in Texas, even before it was an American state, but their role has always shifted based on what was needed from them. Beginning as a militia to protect settlers from Native Americans and themselves (the Rangers have always fought against criminals), they would evolve into the organization that is often mentioned in TV and movies. Though their role in history has sometimes been dubious, and their popularity has been as volatile as the lands that they settled, the Texas Rangers have largely earned their reputation as peaceful lawmen. No organization is perfect, but today, they serve a very important role in law enforcement as a part of the Texas Department of Public Safety. They are called to investigate unsolved crimes, corruption, and shootings involving officers. Just like in the beginning, they serve many different roles to serve the public today.

Chapter 1 – Stephen Austin and the Founding of the Texas Rangers

It is difficult to imagine the early history of this famous (sometimes infamous) organization. Started by an American who had settled in Texas following Mexico's invitation to the Americans to settle the lands, it was meant to provide the kind of protection that was lacking in settlements outside of US territories as the Spanish, then the Mexicans, largely left the settlers to protect themselves.

The American who founded the Texas Rangers was Stephen Fuller Austin. Today, he is known as the Father of Texas, in part because of his role in helping Texas rebel against Mexico but also because of his dedication to ensuring the settlers who lived in the future US state were safe.

The Early Life of Stephen Austin

Born in southwestern Virginia in 1793, Stephen Fuller Austin was born into a family of privilege. As the firstborn son, he was expected to take over the family business, which was in the mining sector. When he was just five years old, his family moved to Missouri. At the young age of eleven, his parents sent him to live with relatives in Connecticut to get an education that would prepare him for the future they envisioned for their eldest son. Austin attended the Bacon Academy, with a focus on English, Latin, Greek, geography, geometry, logic, rhetoric, and writing. Upon his graduation in 1810, Austin moved to Lexington, Kentucky, to attend Transylvania University. He earned a certificate from the school in 1810 and returned to Ste. Genevieve, Missouri.

After his return home, Austin would take on a number of different occupations in addition to working in his family's business. His time serving in a prominent role in his family business required additional training, so Austin received an informal education from his family in how to manage the business. When the US fought in the War of 1812, Austin went to New Orleans and worked as a shipment lead. During this time, he contracted malaria, a disease that causes problems for the rest of the sufferer's life. After this, Austin served as a militiaman in today's state of Illinois. Austin would learn to treat the native population terribly, as the militia's primary job was in harassing the people whose land the settlers were stealing.

Not content to continue to run his father's business, Austin ran for a legislative seat in Missouri during 1815. He was elected and began his service in the Missouri Congress in December of that year.

The family business ended up failing, so the family moved west. Austin's father, Moses, loved the open terrain and beauty of the territory. However, he was also heavily in debt. Some historians say that the move to Spanish Texas was part of a scheme to escape the heavy debt he had accumulated. Moses could not simply move settlers into the area because it was a part of another country; as such, permission was required, so he came up with a plan to approach Governor Antonio Mariá Martínez to allow him to bring settlers into the northern territory of Mexico. After receiving permission through an agreement that was backed by Spain, Moses, his family, and other settlers began their trip to the territory around the end of 1820, even as the Mexican War of Independence raged on. This would come to be a problem the next year when Mexico won the war, but Moses would not be the one to request permission from Mexico to settle the lands. This was left to his son, Stephen Austin, because Moses had contracted pneumonia when he was returning to his family to tell them he had received permission to settle in the territory. He did not live to see the settlement's success as he died in 1821. Stephen Austin went on to complete his father's wish, though not without considerable effort and issues.

Moses Austin had managed to get a grant to settle up to three hundred Americans on 200,000 acres in the northern Mexican territory. Austin led the settlers to the modern-day Brazos and Colorado Rivers, reaching the region in late 1821 or early 1822. Settling was hardly their greatest problem, though, as Spain had lost all claims to the region.

Growing Troubles in the Settlements

The Mexican War of Independence began in 1810, with a Catholic priest named Miguel Hidalgo y Costilla being the one to call for change. Mexico would finally win its independence on September 28th, 1821 (not May 5th as many people believe—this is a date celebrated today because of a victory against the French in 1862). The new country had finally overcome what they considered to be the oppressive rule of Spain, which started less than fifty years after the US had broken away from England. Some say that Hidalgo was inspired by the actions of the French Revolution, though, not the victory of Mexico's northern neighbor.

While this was good for Mexico, it meant that Austin would need to renegotiate the terms and conditions for the settlement, which was still in its early days. When Moses had made an agreement about settling the territory, it had been approved by Spain, and so, Mexico would not acknowledge the agreement that had been made. Stephen Austin's time in the Missouri legislature helped, as he was able to negotiate the continuation of the settlement.

However, the problems were far from over as the new country was in the grip of a power struggle. A Mexican general named Agustín de Iturbide claimed the title of emperor for himself after the end of the war, but he ended up being a very unpopular figure because of the extravagant lifestyle he attempted to lead in a fledgling nation. Mexicans quickly began to back the far more familiar historical figure to people today, Antonio López de Santa Anna. This inner turmoil was finally resolved in the spring of 1823 when Iturbide abdicated his throne.

Not only did Stephen Austin have to deal with the volatile situation in Mexico, but he also had to deal with the Native Americans, who were constantly attacking the settlers, as they had never bothered to try to negotiate with the Comanche and other native peoples. Trying to see to all of the needs of the settlers while protecting them from a wide range of threats meant that Austin's finances were stretched nearly to the breaking point.

In addition to this, Austin was responsible for those who wanted to immigrate into the land Mexico had allowed them to settle. The Mexican government did not want too many foreigners populating their lands, but they did not have the bandwidth to provide any legal assistance or protection to the incoming people. All of the necessities were instead Austin's responsibility to fulfill. From creating all of the social infrastructure —from roads and schools to granaries and sawmills—to law enforcement and land distribution, Austin was pulled in many different directions in the early years of the settlement.

Perhaps the most difficult position he held was in dealing with the Mexican government, though. Mexico was not able to help the settlers, but they still expected the settlers to follow Mexican laws. This included a ban on slavery, something that the settling Americans refused to relinquish. Despite the desire to keep all people marginally free in Mexico, Austin was able to negotiate for the Americans to keep their slaves after the Mexican government banned the institution in 1829.

However, over time, many Americans began to feel that the Mexican rule was becoming oppressive. Some wanted to negotiate new terms, while others wanted to see Texas entirely split from the country and become its own nation. Austin was in favor of remaining as a part of Mexico.

The Growing Need for Law and Order

Amidst all of these growing problems, Austin was forced to look for a way to protect the people without detracting from the incredible load he carried on his shoulders. The most immediate problem after the initial settlement came from the native populations. The primary tribes that continually attacked and raided American settlements were the Camanche, Karankawa, and Tonkawa. While Austin was limited in what he could do to counter these attacks, Mexico did allow him to establish a militia to fight raiding native peoples, as well as to patrol the lands and arrest criminals.

While Austin was in Mexico City working to safeguard the rights to continue to settle, one of his lieutenants, Moses Morrison, began to form a militia to protect the settlers. Asking for ten men to rise to the occasion, he assembled a small contingent to go to the Texas coast, where the Karankawa and Tonkawa tribes were continually attacking the settlers.

When Austin returned, he doubled the number of the militia to twenty. Each of the members of the militia was paid fifteen dollars a month, which was often paid in property instead of money. These twenty men would be the first members of the organization that would come to be known as the Texas Rangers.

In the early days, men were asked to rise to different needs, so the militia was not permanent. When their services were not needed, the volunteers would be disbanded so that they could do what needed to be done for their families. No one moved to this region to serve strictly as military men, so it was not possible to keep the forces for longer than was necessary. They also did not go by the name that is currently used to refer to them; instead, they went by many different names, such as minutemen, scouts, and spies. Nor were they picky about who joined, with Hispanic, Anglo, and native people all serving a wide variety of roles. Until 1835, these men primarily served as protectors when needed. That would all change, though, when the desire for Texas independence boiled over and a different struggle required a more dedicated force of men.

The Latter Years of Stephen Austin

Following the Mexican call to stop all further settlers from entering the American settlement, Americans began to call for a rebellion. An adept politician, Austin was able to make use of a loophole, which continued to allow settlers into the region. This negated Mexico's hope to limit how much influence the settlers would have in the Mexican territory. As more people entered the area, the sentiment for independence grew.

It fell on Austin to try to placate the growing call, something that was proving to be increasingly difficult as he was not in favor of Texas independence. When he did not prove amenable to their demands, some of the settlers drafted their own constitutions and proposed it at the Convention of 1833 in San Felipe. Here, they proposed the name of Texas for the newly independent state. As the representative for the settlers, Austin had to take this and a list of the settlers' demands to Mexico City to present them to Santa Anna.

This move was met with mixed results, as Santa Anna decided to repeal the ban on further settlers from entering the area while denying the request for statehood. This meant that more Americans could continue to move to the area. However, not becoming a state was a major blow to Austin, and Santa Anna compounded the problem when he decided to make an example of the representative for the settlers. Blaming Austin for what appeared to be an insurrection in the settlement, Santa Anna had him imprisoned until

July 1835. Despite this, Austin was still largely against the idea of independence since that had never been his father's goal.

After losing to the settlers in their demand for independence, Austin joined the Texas Revolution in October 1835. At the end of the year, he went to Washington, DC, to request additional support. Since the settlers were American, he hoped to gain military support based on the young US government's desire to protect its own people. However, he also suggested annexing the territory to the US, perhaps as a way to convince them that they had another stake in the fight. Knowing that more was required than the input of politicians, Austin sought to win favorable opinions with the public. Giving speeches as he traveled, the settlement's representative worked hard to encourage the revolution he was so against in the first place.

Initially, his pleas were unsuccessful, and Austin returned to the settlers in 1836. The war had ended shortly before his arrival, and they were in the process of forming a government. Austin would fail to become the newly independent state's first president, losing to the equally famous Sam Houston. This proved to be for the best, though, as Austin became the first secretary of state, albeit for a very short period of time. The election for the presidency was decided in the fall of 1836, soon after Austin became the secretary of state. He did not see any real progress in the new state, though, as he died at the end of December 1836.

Chapter 2 – Growing Discontentment in Texas and the War for Texas Independence

Less than three decades after the Mexicans rebelled against Spain, settlements in the northern part of Mexico rebelled against Mexico. Stipulations had been made prior to the arrival of the settlers, but Mexico did not have time to enforce them. As a result, the northern territories grew and evolved separately from the new country of Mexico.

As unrest grew into resentment, Stephen Austin was constantly on the losing side of trying to keep the settlers and Mexicans from fighting. After roughly a decade, the tensions erupted into the Texas Revolution. The Texas Rangers switched from acting as protectors against the native population and criminals to essentially being outlaws themselves. The territory known as Mexican Texas became their first battleground, changing the way the settlers viewed the organization.

The Ignored Stipulations and Initial Problems

When Moses Austin was given permission to move settlers into the region, Spain had made several stipulations that the settlers had to meet in order to be allowed onto the land. Since Spain was one of the last strongholds of the once-powerful Roman Catholic Church, Spain required that all settlers renounce their religion and convert to Catholicism. They were to become practicing Roman Catholics, something that went against the religious freedom that the settlers were accustomed to as Americans.

The second stipulation was that all settlers would willingly renounce their American citizenship. The settlers would become Mexicans, though they would be differentiated from the natural Mexican citizens by being given the name Tejanos, and they would also have fewer rights than the natural citizens. They were to trade primarily with Mexico, though this was not a rule that was specified in the beginning.

The final requirement was that all settlers would either free their slaves or leave them behind in the United States. Slavery was illegal in Mexico, and they did not want the institution to be brought into their territories by Americans, even though it would continue, and the Mexicans would largely ignore it for a while.

Though these were all requirements that Moses agreed to, and that his son was responsible for ensuring were followed, neither Spain nor Mexico had the time or ability to enforce these stipulations. They were too busy with the war to pay attention to the Americans moving into their territory. Because of this, the settlers ignored the agreements, retaining their nationality, religions, and slaves. Since they would become accustomed to living their lives as they saw fit, they did not welcome the changes that would come after the Mexican War of Independence ended and Mexico began to try to exert stricter control over the territory.

Mexico and the Newly Independent Texas, 1838
(*Source: https://www.raremaps.com/gallery/detail/37793/*
a-map-of-mexico-and-the-republic-of-texas
-1838-niles-pease)

Aftereffects of the Mexican War of Independence

When Mexico finally won its independence, they wanted to ensure that the rule in all of their territories and lands were followed, including the agreement made with Moses Austin. Stephen Austin agreed to work out a new agreement with the new government. The Mexican government wanted a new agreement, but at the same time, it was more than happy to let Americans settle in the territory. The lands were populated with Native Americans who were not welcoming of invaders on their land, and they did not recognize Mexico as owning their lands (just as they had not acknowledged the theft of the lands by Spain). Mexico had too many problems to contend with to quell the threat that the native peoples posed, and of equal concern was the presence of the United States. Mexico feared that the more established nation would attempt to take their land as it continued to expand west. They had already purchased a wide swath of land with the Louisiana Purchase.

Mexico thought that by allowing the American settlers to reside in the region, it would solve both issues. The settlers would be able to distract the native population, so the native peoples would become an American problem. The Mexicans also thought that they would be better able to control the Americans; however, this quickly proved to be untrue as the Americans would be far more difficult to manage than the natives.

Members of the Mexican government and empresarios (Texas land agents—Stephen Austin was one of the empresarios) worked out an agreement that was fairly similar to the one made with Spanish representatives. According to the agreement with Mexico, three hundred Americans would be allowed to settle in the region in the name of Mexico. They would serve as a resource for the new country, developing closer ties to Mexico than the US.

Austin agreed to the conditions, something that was almost certain to happen as the three hundred families had already arrived in the region before the Mexican War for Independence was won (they had arrived earlier in 1821). The initial agreement between Austin and the Mexican government is kept safely in the Texas General Land Office archives. These original settlers would come to be fondly remembered as the "Old Three Hundred." Each of the families who moved to the region was allowed to settle on 4,605 acres. Austin would be given more land, though, as he was not only the empresario of the settlement, but he was also responsible for managing the settlers. He was expected to execute all of the requirements that the Mexican government sent and ensure that Mexican laws were followed.

Many of the original settlers did renounce their American citizenship; however, giving up their slaves was not something they would consider. The vast majority of the first three hundred settlers came from the southeast and had been cotton farmers. Doing all of the hard work that was necessary to farm the bottomlands that rested between the Brazos and Colorado Rivers was not something that the settlers had even considered, not when they were accustomed to having slaves do that kind of work for them. It should be noted that not all of the settlers had slaves, but many of them did. Unfortunately, Mexico gave the new settlers a temporary exception that allowed them to bring their slaves to work the lands in the early days. This exception was only granted in the Texas-Mexico territory, treating the American settlers there differently than other people in Mexico, as well as setting up expectations that the settlers would be able to get what they wanted.

Mexico was not able to provide much support or enforce laws in the territories, relying on the empresarios to follow through with the terms of settling on Mexican lands. They had won their independence at a very high cost both in lives and resources, and the new country was facing serious financial devastation when the war ended in 1821. The mines that had once produced a considerable amount of money under Spanish control were not nearly as efficient under the new government. Food production was also significantly reduced, as Mexicans sought to earn more money in other areas. Unemployment was another significant problem because there was not enough money in circulation to pay workers, which further drove people to relocate in the hopes of finding work and a livelihood. The unrest and problems were only further exacerbated by the large disparity in class within the fledgling country.

The people who rose to different positions within the government had very little experience in governing, so they were not prepared to deal with the rising problems. This led to the wealthy, religious figures, and military leaders stepping into more prominent roles in an effort to retain the class structure that had existed under Spanish rule. While they had wanted freedom from Spain, most of the people in these three classes did not want equality. By ensuring that the antebellum order continued in the new country, the gentry, church officials, and military leaders would have equal control over the direction of the government—much more than they would have had if Spain had continued to control the region. To all parties with power in Mexico, the American settlers seemed to be the perfect solution to help improve the financial situation in the country while protecting the country from the US.

In 1824, the national colonization law was passed, and it was meant to supersede the older imperial colonization law that changed the way the Mexican territory would be populated. Instead of dealing with the Mexican government directly, people wishing to establish new contracts to settle in the territory would need to go directly to the state legislature to make an agreement. Many of the states hoped that they could somehow have greater control over themselves, similar to how the US states largely had control over themselves with minimal interference from the federal government. While the 1824 Federal Constitution of the United Mexican States took a lot of inspiration from the Constitution of the United States of America, it also included some of the tenets that had been written in the Spanish constitution of 1812.

This change would prove to be significant, as the state was better able to monitor the settlers than the Mexican government. They also took a greater interest in who was settling their lands.

Under the Rule of the Coahuila State

Following the passing of the new law, government leaders met in Saltillo to pass the rules for how they would determine who could settle the lands and what requirements must be followed. For the settlers, this meant dealing with the capital city of Saltillo in Coahuila. It was the officials in this capital who would set the requirements and define the terms of any agreement with the empresarios in Texas. This meant that they would also determine who would receive the contracts, whether they were American, European, or Mexican. These were documented in the state colonization law. The focus of the government leaders was largely on ranching and farming in an effort to produce more food and encourage the growth of commerce in the region among the different settlements. According to the new law, Mexicans would have the first choice in settling the northern region, then Americans would be allowed to settle. Initially, immigrants would not be taxed as they strove to establish themselves. They would be required to pay for the lands where they settled, though. In exchange for these fairly minimal requirements, all settlers in the state of Coahuila would have to take an oath saying that they would follow all federal and state laws as laid out in their respective constitutions. They would also have to become Christians if they were not already (though not specifically Roman Catholic). Finally, settlers would swear to act morally and would conduct themselves in a way that reflected strong moral principles.

Once the oath was completed, settlers became naturalized Mexicans.

Texas in the State of Coahuila, 1834
(*Source:https://en.wikipedia.org/wiki/Coahuila_y_Tejas#/media/File: Hooker_Map_of_the_State_of_Coahuila_and_Texas _1834_UTA.jpg*)

The first major issue with this new governmental structure for the established settlers was in their approach to slavery. Since the laws about it were less clear when it came to settlers, Coahuila allowed for slavery to continue within its borders.

Problems began to arise when the federal government began to take a closer look at how the immigrants were doing in following the oath. Many of the Americans were failing to live up to the few requirements of the oath, retaining their own traditions instead of integrating with the Mexican traditions and people. More egregiously, they did not adopt Mexican laws in their settlements. They had blatantly disregarded the laws that were inconvenient to their way of life and implemented their own local laws instead, some of which contradicted Mexican laws.

Rumblings of Independence and Growing Texan Resentment

Nearly a decade before Texas instigated a war for independence, other American settlers were already expressing a desire to revolt against the Mexican government, with the first occurring under Haden Edwards. The settlers in Edward's Colony declared their independence, calling their land the Republic of Fredonia, in 1826. They had planned to work with the Cherokees, forming an alliance and creating a new flag representing the Americans and native peoples. After signing a declaration of independence in December of 1826, they turned to the US for support. They also asked Austin to assist them in their fight against the Mexican government. Predictably, Austin sided with the Mexican government, and he came to join the Mexicans in putting down the rebellion. By the end of January 1827, the Republic of Fredonia was no more. Unhappy that they had been dragged into such a poorly planned rebellion, the Cherokees killed the main leaders, John Dunn Hunter and Richard Fields. Haden Edwards survived and would later join the war Texas Revolution.

Mexico was understandably shaken by this apparently unprovoked call for independence. They became warier and did want to allow any further American settlers into their territories. Since it had been the responsibility of the federal government, not the state government, to put down the rebellion, the Mexican government began to try to consolidate power. They wanted to build a much stronger central government that was more closely aligned with the way that Spain ruled. So, they began drafting new laws toward the end of 1829 and passed them in April of 1830. The new laws voided any existing agreement with the settlers if the settlers were not complying with the terms of the new agreement, in addition to curtailing American immigration. The only exceptions to this were the settlements under Stephen Austin and Green DeWitt. The Mexican government found that these two empresarios had fulfilled their requirements (something that was not completely true for either of the two men). The Mexican government further established military outposts so they could ensure that American settlers did not continue to enter Mexico. No more slaves could be brought into the country either, though slaves who already resided in the country could remain enslaved.

For the last five years prior to the new agreement, both Coahuila and the American settlers had greatly benefited from the relationship they had established. In fact, they were prospering in a way that had eluded much of the rest of Mexico. Commerce had become stable and was even lucrative in some regions. The federal government's interference threatened both the free commerce that had been established, as well as the sovereignty of Coahuila. Slaves had also been allowed to be brought into Coahuila because there were not enough people to work the lands without them. However, they were to be indentured and have the ability to earn money to buy their own freedom. Under the new laws, though, that would no longer be possible, and people in the Texan territory feared that would further reduce their ability to conduct commerce while stunting growth. It was suspected that completely eliminating the ability to bring any more slaves into Mexico was meant to be a further deterrent for the kinds of Americans who often came. If they could not bring their slaves, they would not be tempted to enter the country, or at least that was the supposition. The rise of anti-immigration laws resulted in much greater hostility between the Anglo-Americans and Mexicans. It did not have the desired effect of cooling the situation.

Santa Anna took action in 1833 to alleviate the issue. He led the government in revoking the law that had institutionalized immigration discrimination, and the effects were nearly immediate, as Americans began to immigrate into the regions that had been prospering under the better-established settlements. Roughly a year later, Santa Anna would reverse his decision to allow greater states' rights. He called for the congregation of a new congress that would create a strong central government. It took nearly a year, but the country was reconfigured in the fall of 1835, with states being converted into departments that would then be controlled by president appointees.

This did not sit well with the people in Coahuila, particularly the people in Austin's settlement. Mexico was embroiled in a civil war at the time, which made it the opportune time for Texans to finally break from the nation that had invited them to settle the lands that actually belonged to the Native Americans.

Rebellion and Independence

Fearing the rise of the settlers, the Mexican commander in the region requested reinforcements to quell the unrest. Word spread that a military force was being raised against them, and William B. Travis led a group of Texans to attack Anahuac in June 1835. When they refused to surrender, Mexico took this as a direct rebellion against Mexican laws. In 1836, the Texas Declaration of Independence was signed by 59 men, three of whom were Mexican descendants.

The first real conflict in the fight for Texan independence was at the Battle of Gonzales in October of 1835. The rebels won, and they were able to block the Mexican forces at the Gulf of Mexico so that they could not provide new supplies to their forces.

By 1836, the Texas Revolution had begun, and it was going well for the Texans almost from the beginning. This was the first recorded instance where the Texas Rangers received a government sanction to patrol the frontiers against the Native Americans since they continued to be a problem, particularly while the Texans were preoccupied with fighting the Mexican government. Some of the members of the Rangers had also fought against the Mexican government, but most of the forces worked to protect the settlers while others fought in the war for Texan independence. As they were adept trackers, some of the Rangers were called on to act as scouts. Also, because they were familiar with the lands, others served as carriers.

After the disaster at the Alamo (in modern-day San Antonio) in March 1836, the Rangers went to help the Texans fleeing from the area. They assisted in getting settlers to safety and destroyed anything left behind so that it could not be used by the Mexicans, including produce. When the Rangers were called to act as escorts at the Battle of San Jacinto in April 1836, many of the Rangers were annoyed with their role. Many of them preferred either to fight in the war against the Mexicans or against the Native Americans. The menial tasks assigned to them during the war seemed to be a step down from their usual duties, which had been important when the area was a part of Mexican Texas.

However, their role would begin to undergo a significant shift following the close of the war, in large part because they became the only established law enforcement group in Texas. How the Rangers would be used by the new government would differ depending on the governor in charge, but their place and role in the new country began to solidify once they were one of the few established forces in Texas.

Chapter 3 – Protecting New Settlers after the Revolution

Once the Texas Revolution ended, the role of the Texas Rangers became critical to the protection of the settlers, especially since they moved to the new country in droves. For the first time in its history, the Texas Rangers were more than just a force made of volunteers called to protect; they became a permanent protective force to monitor the borders.

A New Standing Force

When they had been part of Mexican Texas, the Texas Rangers had served two primary purposes: fighting Native Americans and dealing with criminals. There were times when the Rangers would act as judge, jury, and executioner, something that was accepted by the settlers because they did not have any other established justice system. The Rangers were only called to serve when there was a need. Otherwise, the Rangers worked on farms and as merchants. For their service, the Rangers were paid very little because the settlement could not afford to pay them much. The territory certainly could not afford its own standing military force.

This quickly changed, however, once Texas became its own country, known as the Republic of Texas. Once the war for their independence ended, Texans needed to create all of the branches of government, as well as a military. While they had been wealthier than much of Mexico, Texas had been a territory with many settlements, with Stephen Austin's being one of the largest. Once the Texas military was dissolved when the war ended, the new government knew that they would need to keep some kind of military and law enforcement working for the country. Now they not only had to be careful of the native population around them, but they also had a new enemy in the country they had just revolted against: Mexico.

However, while the Rangers had worked as military men to some extent, they had not worked in a way that was conducive to military service. Their role had always been much closer to law enforcement and protection. Although they had been sanctioned during the Texas Revolution, their largest role during the war had been to patrol the frontier, not participate in the fighting. Since Mexico did not have the means to continue to fight the Texans after the war, the primary threat for the new Texas nation was still the native peoples. This was a threat that the Rangers knew how to face, though.

The Texas Rangers were a permanent organization, but Texas could not afford to pay men to be dedicated all of the time. Because the government was still looking for its footing, the Texas Rangers continued to largely be men who volunteered to serve. When they were needed, they would be called up to work along the borders and frontier. Once the threat was resolved, the Texas Rangers disbanded. However, this would change, particularly with the boom of new settlers looking to take advantage of the newly liberated region.

Changes to the Rangers

From the beginning, the Texas Rangers were made of an interesting mix of men. There was no requirement for the volunteer organization, so it included former Americans, Mexicans, and Native

Americans. Each of them brought a wealth of specific knowledge with them, which was what made the Texas Rangers so reliable in the early days. Their reputation as efficient and effective protectors was only increased following the war, in large part because they had been responsible for protecting the people. When families were forced to move, it was the Rangers who came in and helped them relocate. This relationship was what helped to ensure that the organization continued even after the war ended.

With men who already knew how to protect the people, scout, hunt, and serve the public, the Texas Rangers quickly became essential to the Texas government. Considering one of the reasons that Texas revolted from Mexico was because of the way the new policies negatively affected immigration, the new government wanted to make sure to assuage settlers' fears about moving to Texas. Once the barrier imposed by Mexico was removed by winning their independence, Texas was not ready for the deluge of immigrants wanting to settle in the newly freed lands. From having too few people arriving in order to prosper to having more than they could safely protect, Texas became reliant on the Texas Rangers to ensure that the settlers were safe.

The large influx of new settlers flooding into the region caused even greater tension between the native peoples and the new nation. People began to try to settle the lands Texas sold them that actually belonged to the native peoples. This caused a significant increase in open hostilities, and Texas did not have many resources to face the growing threat. So, the Texas Rangers were charged with serving as a patrol along the borders of both the frontier, where the native peoples were, and along the border with Mexico.

Initially, the first president, Sam Houston, sought to establish a peaceful coexistence with the native peoples. He wanted to work with them to build a strong economy (there was little chance of this happening with Mexico, and the US had not offered help during their war for independence). Considering the Native Americans knew the area far better than any of the settlers, it made sense to foster a good relationship with them. Had his policies been continued after he left his position, things might have turned out differently. However, in 1838, Mirabeau Lamar became the new president of the Republic of Texas, and he did not agree with the direction Houston had taken.

Upon taking office, Lamar made significant changes to the frontier policies, and the Rangers were charged with implementing these changes. It was not possible to accomplish what Lamar wanted with the small contingent of Rangers who served only when needed. So, the Texas Congress passed legislation allowing the new president to form a larger company of men. This new, more robust Texas Rangers organization had eight companies, each full of mounted volunteers. There would also be a company consisting of 56 Rangers that would be maintained (they were not volunteers). A month after forming these nine companies, the Rangers would continue to add new companies to cover central and southern Texas.

Once they had a more militant structure, the Rangers began to openly fight with the native peoples, waging war for three years against the people whose lands the Texans continued to steal. This was a complete corruption of their original purpose, as they were no longer protecting the people but provoking wars.

Chapter 4 –Driving the Natives from Their Homes

With their new purpose clear, the Texas Rangers waged almost continual warfare for three years against the people who had rightful claims to the land. President Lamar wanted to entirely remove the Native American peoples from their own ancestral lands so that white settlers could take over and prosper. Perhaps he hoped that by removing the native people, they would no longer have to worry about patrolling their borders. However, he clearly neglected to consider that there was a much larger threat just south of the Texas border. The war that Lamar insisted be waged against the indigenous population would end up encouraging the Mexicans to help the native peoples as a way to weaken Texas, and this policy eventually lost Lamar the presidency.

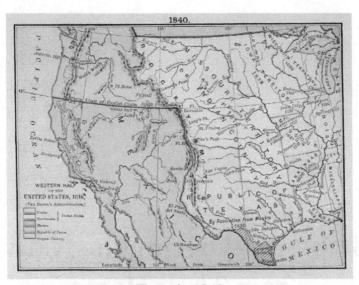

Texas in 1840
(*Source: https://truthhugger.files.wordpress.com/ 2007/09/repubtxmap.jpg*)

Unfortunately, the three years and the three major battles were detrimental to the Native Americans, and by the time the wars ended, there were no strong tribes remaining to stop the further advancement of Texans into their lands.

The Cherokee War

The problem between the native peoples and the settlers stemmed from agreements made long before Texas became independent. The Spanish had given the natives the rights to their own lands without taxing them. During February 1836, the two primary representatives of the provisional government of Texas (Sam Houston and John Forbes) had signed a treaty with the Cherokees and the tribes associated with them, granting the tribes the region spanning between the Angelina and Sabine Rivers. At the end of that same year, the newly elected Texas Senate tabled the treaty. Instead of ratifying it, they voided it in December 1837.

The Nacogdoches area of Texas was primarily populated by people of Mexican descent, and they were upset with the revolution that removed the territory from their country. When the Texas Revolution ended, the inhabitants that were of Mexican descent were further angered when Americans began trekking into and squatting on their lands. Those of Mexican descent had good reason to align with the Cherokees, as they had been friendly with both the Spanish and the Mexicans than the American settlers. Vicente Córdova was a Mexican loyalist who remained in contact with the country of Mexico and began a rebellion in 1838. Since the Cherokee had aligned with him, Texans sent Thomas Jefferson Rusk and their military against Córdova's forces, hoping to intercept Córdova. He managed to elude the force, who then returned to their homes.

The Texans then marched against the natives in 1838, attacking the Kickapoos. In response, the Native Americans conducted a series of raids from the end of 1838 to the beginning of 1839. During this time, the Texans learned that the Mexican government was trying to persuade the Native Americans in the Texas area to rise up against the Texans. President Lamar took this news and used it to justify the full removal of the native peoples from their own land, not bothering to find out which—or even if—the Native Americans had agreed to act against them. In the summer of 1839, a troop of five hundred men was sent to force the Cherokee out of Texas and into the Arkansas Territory.

Cherokee Chief Bowl went to discuss the removal of his people from the lands on July 12th, 1838. An agreement was struck that the Cherokee and their associated tribes would be allowed to profit from the crops they had grown and that Texas would cover the cost for their movement out of the region. When the Texans insisted that they be allowed to send an armed escort to oversee the removal, the Cherokee refused to sign the treaty. Three days after Chief Bowl arrived to negotiate, the Texans declared they were marching on a nearby Cherokee village to enact the removal without an agreement. They told the Cherokee that any of their tribe who was willing to leave needed to have a white flag outside of their home. Otherwise, they would be attacked.

The Texans sent a contingent of men to the village to cut off any of the Cherokee who sought to leave without the escort. They met with Cherokee attempting to flee at Neches, which was when the Battle of the Neches began. The Texans killed or wounded an estimated one hundred natives while losing five of their own men and fewer than thirty being injured. The Cherokees, Kickapoos, Delawares, and Shawnees all lost people in the battle, and they were removed from the region following the end of the Cherokee War in 1839.

After the Cherokee War, the only two tribes that had a significant population in the region of Texas were the Alabama and the Coushatta. The other eastern Texan tribes were completely removed by the end of 1839. Under President Lamar, Texas was proving to have adapted an eradication policy, regardless of the services and assistance that the natives had given the settlers. The first war of removal had been successful, encouraging Lamar and those who sided with him that they could ultimately turn Texas into a place where only Americans would be welcomed.

The Council House Fight

The relationship between the Comanche and the Texans had always been tense, with skirmishes being common. Each side attacked and raided against the other for years, but it wasn't until March 1840 when the sides became openly hostile.

At the beginning of 1840, the Penatekas, a part of the Comanche people, sought to make a treaty with Texas. Their population had been decimated by smallpox, and they were an easy target for the Cheyenne and Arapaho. The Texas Rangers had been the most immediate problem, having successfully and repeatedly attacked the Penatekas based on their president's policies toward the native people in the region. The Penateka representatives arrived to negotiate peace in San Antonio sometime in January 1840. In response to the arrival of the natives, the government made three demands against the Comanche. Firstly, the Comanche must immediately release all of the captives that the Penatekas were currently holding. Second, they had to leave their ancestral lands, which the Texans now claimed as their own, and had to avoid disturbing the settlers as they left. Third, the Comanche would not interfere with Texas pushing into other territories, as Texas and Mexico were disputing how much land Texas had won during the Texas Revolution.

The first contingent of peace-seeking natives was not able to negotiate favorable conditions, so more representatives were sent to discuss terms. They arrived in March 1840, led by Muk-wah-ruh. The Texans brought them into the Council House to begin discussing the terms that they had offered the first time. The Comanche had brought only a handful of prisoners, including a few Mexican children and a sixteen-year-old Texan named Matilda. She told the Texans that the natives had abused her and that they had left fifteen other prisoners behind with the intention of ransoming them as hostages.

The Texans immediately demanded that the other prisoners be released, to which Muk-wah-ruh said he did not have the authority to release those prisoners, as they were the captives of other Comanche over whom he did not have authority. Utterly failing to grasp the way the Comanche worked, the Texans rejected this explanation, and soldiers were brought into the facility where the negotiations were being held. The Texas government then announced that the people who had come to negotiate peace would be held as their prisoners until all of the prisoners the teenage girl had told them about were released. The Comanche chiefs attempted to escape, even calling for support from the soldiers who had traveled with them and remained outside of the Council House. The soldiers slaughtered the chiefs who were inside while a fight broke out in front of the Council House.

When the fighting was over, 27 Comanche were taken as hostages. The Texans sent a Comanche woman back to her people to tell the remaining leaders that the other hostages would be kept until all of the white prisoners were released.

Outraged that the Texans would undermine peace talks by taking negotiators as prisoners, the Comanche refused to further discuss peace with them. Over time, nearly all of the captive Comanche managed to escape.

The Comanche would remain in the area, brutally attacking and raiding the treacherous Texans. The Council House Fight had taught the Comanche that the Texans would not honor peace talks. Even today, the actions of the Texans would be considered reprehensible, as ambassadors are supposed to be immune from these tactics. Had this happened today, the Texans would have faced sanctions and outrage. As it was, their actions were normal at the time because Americans did not consider talks or war with native peoples as being subject to the rules and regulations that they followed when dealing with Europeans. From this point on, it was a war of attrition, but the Comanche would continue to be a hostile force who posed a real threat to the settlers who pushed into the territories that both Texas and Mexico claimed.

Battle of Plum Creek

Following the Council House Fight, the Comanche began a campaign against the Texans. During the summer of 1840, they conducted a series of raids against settlers in the Guadalupe Valley. They slaughtered settlers in their homes, took anything of value, and left with the horses and livestock that they could handle. They would also burn settlements, leaving a long stretch of burned homes throughout the valley.

The Comanche continued to raid and plunder until reaching Linnville. When Texas sent a force of volunteers, including the Texas Rangers, who were led by Ben McCulloch, the Comanche began to retreat. The Texans were able to catch up to the retreating natives at Plum Creek, where the Texans killed nearly every Comanche in the area.

It was to be the last act of defiance for the Comanche. Following this victory by the Texans, the Comanche did not have many options. With their numbers in decline because of the constant fighting and the smallpox that the Texans carried, the Comanche were finally pushed west.

The policies of Texas under its second president managed to make enemies of everyone around them. It would soon become clear that Texas could not continue to alienate everyone without suffering some serious consequences. The Cherokee had already proved that they were in contact with the Mexicans, even if they were not actively working with Texas' southern neighbors. It was becoming increasingly clear that Texas needed an ally who would trust them, and Texas would not get that from any of the native people around them, especially after the way they had dealt with the Comanche during the peace talks, or from Mexico. That only left the US. With so many of the settlers being American, there was a lot of support in trying to see what kind of agreement Texas could come to with this more powerful nation.

Chapter 5 – The Annexation of Texas

Having alienated nearly every group around them, the Texans knew that it was only a matter of time before their neighbors would band together and snuff out Texas. With retaliation being inevitable, they turned to the one country that they had not yet offended—the United States. It is perhaps ironic that the US was their only option because it was the US who had refused to assist Texas during the Texas Revolution. The Cherokee had actually shown a willingness to work against the Mexicans prior to the revolution. Instead of fostering this relationship, which President Houston had wanted, Texas turned to the nation that had ignored them in their time of need.

With the war roughly a decade in the past, the US no longer saw it as a potential risk, and so, they were finally open to the idea of helping Texas. It would be a messy endeavor, but by the end of the 1840s, Texas would officially become the 28th US state.

The Calm before the Storm

In the years between 1840 and 1845, the Texas Rangers primarily served as protectors from the few remaining tribes who occasionally attacked the settlers. Sam Houston was again elected to be the president in 1841 after Lamar had lost the support he enjoyed previously.

Houston's focus was the same as before: he sought to protect the settlers without trying to instigate wars. The Texas Rangers remained the best method of accomplishing this, as well as being the most cost-effective solution. However, the enemy that concerned Houston the most was Mexico. They had begun to frequently attack Texas along the southern border, particularly as talks of annexation to the US continued. To protect people in the southern regions of Texas, Captain John Coffee Hays took 150 Rangers to the southern border. He had been pivotal in helping defeat the Native Americans, and he proved to be equally adept at repelling the advances of Mexico into Texan territory.

During these trying years, Hays would begin some of the first Ranger traditions, including recruiting new men to the organization. New recruits were provided training in how to fight using guerilla tactics that had proven successful against the opposition. It was Hays's dedication to the Rangers that would make them the force that would continue to thrive even after the US annexed Texas. Hays's training of the new recruits would prove to be critical in the immediate aftermath of the annexation as well. Under his leadership, a number of notable figures in Texas Ranger history (who you can read about in Chapter 10) would begin their illustrious (and sometimes infamous) careers, including the McCulloch brothers, Samuel Walker, and William "Bigfoot" Wallace.

Fulfilling an Earlier Expectation

The idea that Texas would be annexed by the US was not a new one. Stephen Austin had suggested it prior to the end of the Texas Revolution, only to be rejected. Though many Americans had settled onto the Texan lands, those lands still belonged to Mexico. The tensions between the US and Mexico were already great enough that the US was concerned about starting a war with them, resulting in them turning down Austin's offer.

The first official move to join the US came in 1836 with the first election after the Texas Revolution. The people voted in favor of Texas finally being annexed into the US. Although the vote showed that the people were ready for this move, the Texas government failed to complete a treaty with the US that ratified them as a new state. Besides, the US was reluctant to annex lands that had so recently been a part of Mexico.

However, once Texas had succeeded in winning its independence, the US kept an eye on the new nation, weighing its options. With more Americans streaming into Texas, there was also a sense of duty in protecting its citizens. Texas did not force any of the immigrants to renounce their citizenship, so the new settlers were largely American. They continued to expect protection from the US, especially as tensions with the natives and Mexicans mounted. There was ample evidence that Mexico was planning on initiating another attack, with some of the proof coming during the Cherokee War.

The Joint Resolution for Annexing Texas

Though it took nearly a decade, the US government finally reached a resolution that would allow Texas to officially enter the large nation as a state. Over the years, the US government had failed to reach and sign an official treaty with Texas, so they switched to another method of bringing it into the union.

There were several reasons why this took so long. One of the most notable concerns was the debt that Texas had incurred during the war. The settlers had been fairly prosperous under the Mexican government, but they were not wealthy, and the war resulted in a large debt that the US was not willing to take on. Another major issue was the rising division in the US about slavery. Each new territory that was brought into the country had to be assessed by abolitionists and the pro-slave lobbyists to determine whether slavery would be allowed in the future state. Adding Texas would mean giving the pro-slave side a large swath of land, destabilizing the delicate balance. Texans had already proven that they had no intention of giving up their slaves, even convincing the Mexican government to allow it prior to the revolution.

Since the Texas Revolution, Mexico had made it clear that if the US annexed Texas, Mexico would take that as a declaration of war. For this reason, the US avoided any kind of negotiation until 1844. When the US finally started talking to Texas about the annexation, Mexico severed all diplomatic relations. US President John Tyler was unable to get the necessary votes in the Senate to ratify the treaty that had been negotiated with Texas that year. His next bid to annex the nation was in 1845, a few months before he was to leave office.

When the US passed a joint resolution for annexation, the US included three major conditions on the new state. First, Texas would remain in control of its public lands and its debts; the US would not manage them, giving Texas considerable control over its lands. The second condition partly addressed the problem of slavery because if the US decided that it wanted to divide Texas into four new states, it would have the right to do that. Finally, the US government would be responsible for providing governmental facilities, postal services, and military forces, but they would retain authority over the state, as they did in all states in the Union. That meant that Texas could control the lands, but they had to abide by American laws, particularly on the lands where the US government was providing basic services.

By taking on Texas as a state, the US was taking a large risk. They would be helping to build a governmental system that would run and operate based on a much larger network, which would be costly.

The proposal was presented in July 1845 to a group of elected officials at the Constitutional Convention held in Austin. They had proposals to consider, including the joint resolution for its annexation and a peace treaty with Mexico. The peace treaty would finally settle the fight between Texas and Mexico, but it required Texas to remain its own nation. If Texas opted to be annexed to the

US, hostilities would continue. The end vote was exactly what was expected—the representatives voted to do what the Texans had wanted since before the Texas Revolution: be annexed into the US. The proposal was then put to the people in October that same year. The vote to join the US became official when the Annexation Ordinance and a state constitution made the move to US statehood final.

Once Texas submitted their votes to the US, it was sent to Congress, where it was quickly accepted. Before the end of 1845, the joint resolution to admit Texas as a state was put before President James Polk for his signature. After nearly a decade of waiting, Texas was finally a state. The transfer of control began soon after, with the formal transfer occurring in February 1846.

Chapter 6 – The Mexican-American War

The Mexican-American War was something that most people knew was coming; it was more a question of when than if. Mexico and Texas were already disputing where their borders were. If the US were to become a player in that dispute, Mexico knew that they would lose even more territory. Compared to the US, which had largely thrived since their revolution in 1776, Mexico had struggled, with a civil war punctuating their precarious position. Fighting the US was something that Mexico hoped to avoid.

This became impossible because of the events that occurred soon after the annexation of Texas. Despite the people of both nations being against war, the two nations ended up being in one because they each felt that the other had disrespected them. One of the primary justifications was based on what happened in the territory that both sides tried to claim as their own.

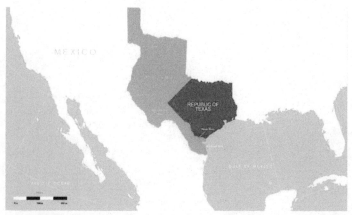

Disputed Lands between Mexico, Texas, and the US
(*Source:https://upload.wikimedia.org/wikipedia/commons/0/09/Rep
ublic_of_Texas_labeled.svg*)

Mexico's Growing Concern

Even before Texas broke from Mexico, Mexican officials were concerned that they would lose territory to the US. Once Texas successfully fought Mexico to gain its independence without the help of the US, Mexico's fear about what could happen intensified. Between 1836 and 1845, Mexico did everything in its power to dissuade the US from annexing land that had so recently belonged to the southern country.

One of the biggest points of contention between Texas and Mexico was how much of the territory belonged to Texas and how much belonged to Mexico. The region in question would have more than doubled Texas. On its own, Texas did not pose much of a threat in forcing Mexico to relinquish the lands. That would change, however, if the US were to annex it. Besides fighting for their new state, Americans under the newly elected President Polk were obviously seeking to bring to fruition the idea of Manifest Destiny. This was the belief that the US was meant to stretch its lands from the Atlantic to the Pacific. The Louisiana Purchase had helped to make this a reality under Thomas Jefferson, but the US was eyeing a lot of Mexican territories in an effort to fulfill what they thought was right and inevitable.

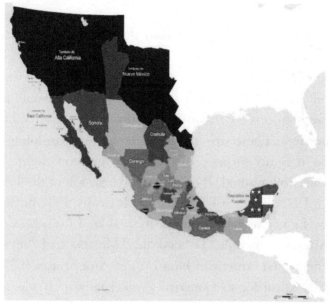

Mexico in 1845: In the Path of US Expansion
(*Source:https://en.wikipedia.org/wiki/Territorial_evolution_of_Mexic o#/media/File:Mapa_Mexico_1845.PNG*)

Initially, there was not much support on either side for war. However, Mexico was in a much weaker position, as they were still attempting to build a nation amid civil wars and other power struggles. The US had been a nation for several decades and had coalesced around a stronger government. The odds against Mexico were very obvious.

By annexing Texas, the US proved that it was finally willing to start fighting to take over Mexican lands because they then claimed to own the disputed lands. Prior to this, the US had actually sent people to negotiate the purchase of a large swath of the northern area of Mexico. John Slidell and a small contingent of politicians went to negotiate the purchase. Trying to replicate the cheap cost that the US had paid with the Louisiana Purchase, which, in theory, more than doubled the size of the US in 1803 for fifteen million dollars or eighteen dollars per square mile, Slidell was authorized to offer thirty million dollars. The Mexican government would not even meet with him, as they had no desire to sell its lands.

When Slidell returned, saying that Mexico was unwilling to meet with him, President Polk decided to turn that into an insult to the nation. Polk then forced a war because he knew that this was the only way to potentially acquire the lands he felt were destined to be a part of the United States. To ensure that the US military would instigate a war, he sent troops to reside in the disputed region south of the Texas border. These troops were technically invading another nation, so it is no surprise that Mexico fired on them. This was exactly what Polk wanted. By warping the invasion of the US into the death of a US soldier on US lands by Mexicans, Polk finally created the excuse he needed to start a war to steal land from Mexico. Lying to the American people, he said that Mexico had "invaded our territory and shed American blood upon American soil." This was followed by an order to Congress to declare war. It was a lie, and there were many Americans who questioned it. Northern states said that Polk, who was a Southerner, was attempting to acquire more slave-holding states and create greater control for slaveholders. There were also a number of Americans who simply did not want to go to war to steal lands from another country, as it had not even been one hundred years since they had won their own freedom. Many people still strongly felt that they should not be the aggressors (except when it came to displacing the Native Americans).

Despite the protests of many Americans about going to war, Congress gave their approval for the war on May 13th, 1846.

The Mexican War

The war would later be described by a young second lieutenant named Ulysses S. Grant as a war that was "one of the most unjust ever waged by a stronger against a weaker nation. It was an instance of a republic following the bad example of European monarchies, in not considering justice in their desire to acquire additional territory."

This was exactly what had made many Americans against the idea of war before it was declared. However, once they were committed, many Americans felt it was necessary to provide support and boost the morale of the soldiers. Even if the war was wrong, the Americans did not blame the soldiers. The Mexicans, on the other hand, were not only against the war, but they were also not in a position where they felt that they could benefit from it. America was an aggressor that had largely been at peace since winning its independence. This was in stark contrast to the chaotic aftermath of the Mexican War of Independence. Their morale was already low, and it was just one more fight, this time against a much more powerful force. The Mexican soldiers and people were just as aware of the superior force of the US as Grant.

There were three notable officers fighting in the Mexican-American War: General Zachary Taylor, Ulysses S. Grant, and Robert E. Lee. For both Grant and Lee, it was their first experience fighting in a war. Despite this and the superior numbers of the Mexicans, the Americans managed to quickly rule the battlefield.

The Mexican-American War began in April 1846 with eight thousand American soldiers. Wanting to provide support and fight for their country, more than sixty thousand Americans soon joined as volunteers. There were over 73,000 Mexicans, who were similarly a mix of regulars and volunteers. The Mexican Navy was also unable to contend with the much more robust US Navy. Polk also sought to sow discontent in the other Mexican territories in California and sent John Fremont and Stephen Kearny to instigate a revolution in the area. The people in California declared themselves the Bear Flag Republic even before they learned of the fighting. Led by Fremont, they marched on the military outpost Mexican Presidio and secured the region for the US. While Fremont was ensuring the theft of the California region, Kearny was enacting a similar strategy in New Mexico, driving the governor out of the region. He and his band captured the capital, and after their success, Kearny led his men west to join with the successful Californians.

As Kearny and Fremont secured the northern region, Generals Zachary Taylor and Winfield Scott marched on Mexico City. Taylor faced Antonio López de Santa Anna directly and headed toward the capital's center, while Scott approached the city from a different angle. Scott and his men successfully took control of the city, leaving the Mexicans with no other option but to surrender in September 1847. This put the US in a much better position to negotiate for the lands at a much lower cost.

Ironically, the annexation of Texas and the Mexican-American War would be two major contributors to the American Civil War. By pushing for something that the majority of Americans did not want, the nation was further divided. Discussions began to spread about Polk's underhanded methods and unconstitutional behavior in essentially forcing the country into an unjustified war.

One of the nation's most notable writers of the time, Henry David Thoreau, would believe so strongly that the war had been wrong that he was arrested for refusing to pay taxes in protest of the war. From his protests came a work that is still used today to enact peaceful change, *Civil Disobedience.*

This was all a prelude for what would come later. The acquisition of so much land by a nation that was already so divided would result in far more internal hostilities. By winning the Mexican-American War, the US all but assured that it would tear itself apart just a couple of decades later. The Missouri Compromise of 1850, which was meant to address the new American lands and if they would be slave states or free states, would ultimately be the undoing of the US for several decades.

Treaty of Guadalupe Hidalgo

It is also ironic that the treaty to end the war was made without the president's knowledge. Signed on February 2nd, 1848, the treaty set the boundaries for the regions that would be a part of the US going forward, including all of the southwestern states of the US today.

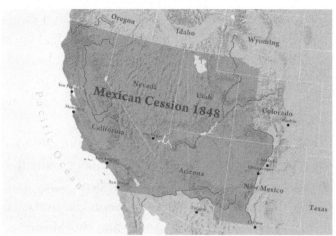

Lands Lost after the Mexican-American War
(*Source:https://en.wikipedia.org/wiki/Mexican_Cession#/media/File: Mexican_Cession.png*)

Mexico received nearly half of what would have been offered them prior to the war, with all of these lands becoming a part of the US for between fifteen and eighteen million dollars (the US also took on some of the Mexican debt for these regions, increasing the cost of the lands). The disputed lands with Texas were definitively identified, and the new borders were drawn. A single war lost Mexico over half of its lands.

Polk endorsed the treaty, then sent it to Congress for final approval. It passed by a vote of 34 to 14 in March 1848

How the Texas Rangers Fought to Ensure US Victory

With the majority of the Americans fighting in the war being volunteers and the rest coming from very different lands, the Texas Rangers were among the few fighters who knew the region and had experience fighting. General Taylor would quickly realize just how instrumental the skills of the Rangers could give the US an advantage. He requested that the Rangers leader, Jack Hays, establish four divisions to go into Mexico. Hays was able to establish three for the war, and they would soon come to be his "eyes and ears" as Hays moved farther into Mexico. The Rangers not only had knowledge of the region and how to survive in the heat, but they also had superior weapons compared to most of the soldiers. They helped to determine the best route into Mexico, and Taylor would use that in his march toward the nation's heart.

Though Scott and his men would push through to the city's center, this was largely possible because of how rapidly the Rangers were able to help Taylor push into Mexico. They had already reached Mexico City by the time of Scott's arrival. They were instrumental in several definitive battles, and the Mexicans came to call the Rangers "Los Diablos Tejanos" or "the Texas Devils." The Rangers usually wore a handkerchief around their necks as a sign of their position. Mexicans despised the men and would immediately become hostile when they arrived in Mexican towns. In one town, a few men threw rocks at the Rangers. In response, the three men were immediately shot without any warning.

While the Rangers were certainly brutal in their response, they also provided a lot of protection for American soldiers. When US soldiers began to be killed in the red-light district of a local town, Taylor brought it to Hays's attention. In response, he had the Rangers set up traps to find out which locals were killing the American soldiers. No more US soldiers died after the Rangers got involved, while 83 Mexicans were killed. The Rangers didn't lose any men.

Texas had not been a part of the US for long when the Mexican-American War began. This meant that the Rangers had continued to play a pivotal role in protecting the people. However, once the war was over, the US government was able to begin implementing its own rules and laws in the region. This led to the decline of the Rangers as they were no longer needed to act in defense of the settlers and borders. They were more of an auxiliary than a necessity, and Texas largely stopped enlisting people into the organization. Apart from occasional fights with the native peoples, the Rangers did not have much of a role in the state, so they lost many of their best leaders and fighters. Even during the American Civil War, they did not have much of a role to play as most of the fighting occurred in the southeastern states. Without the rise of some famous criminals, the Texas Rangers may have entirely disappeared, particularly given their less than positive image over the next few decades.

Chapter 7 – Corruption, Loss of Popularity, Rebuilding and Restoring an Earlier Image

With the US taking control of a lot of the previous work that the Texas Rangers were initially formed to do, the Rangers were not needed in the same way as before. This led to them being somewhat divided and uncertain in how they would work for the next few decades. Their importance in the Mexican-American War, coupled with their role as protectors, made them popular with the people. However, without their single purpose anymore, the Texas Rangers began to become more of a problem.

Resumption of Patrols

While there were a lot of things that the US government took control over, Texas was still responsible for some of its own protection. This left some of the old familiar tasks that the Texas Rangers had been doing for years, but it also limited what they could do. They were no longer enforcing their own laws, though, and being regulated was not something they were accustomed to.

While they still had some work in protecting the people of Texas from the Native Americans, they primarily tracked down cattle rustlers and thieves. Perhaps the Rangers were emboldened by the new backing of the US, or it is possible that they felt that they had earned a name that made them impervious to criticism. It is certain that many of the more notable members left after the war, and it is possible that many of the remaining members were more concerned with power than with doing what was right.

Whatever the reason, the Texas Rangers became noticeably more aggressive after the war. They seemed to continue some of the policies that started under President Lamar. Instead of protecting Americans from the native peoples, they actively attacked the Native Americans. They would stalk the native peoples, monitoring their movements before attacking. The majority of Texans may not have had a problem when the Texas Rangers turned against the native peoples, but they would look less favorably on the Rangers when the native population was nearly gone and the aggression was turned against the Texans.

It would take a few years before the Rangers had reduced the native population to numbers where they couldn't pose any kind of a threat. The first campaign began soon after the Mexican-American War ended. Led by a Ranger known as John Salmon "Rip" Ford, roughly one hundred Rangers began a campaign against the few remaining Comanche who were not driven out when Texas first became a nation of its own. Members of the Tonkawa tribe joined the Rangers in fighting their long-time enemies. The Rangers and Tonkawa were told by the politicians that they were to punish the Comanche for raids that they had carried out over the years, even if the Comanche had not been very active since their numbers had been significantly reduced. Though they had been ordered to remove the Comanche, the attackers had not been given permission to go beyond the established boundaries, though. Ignoring the established territories and agreements with the Comanche, the Rangers conducted raids in Comanche territories, effectively invading another nation. Unlike with the Mexican-American War, the Rangers did not have permission to go to war. This was only one of the first instances where the Rangers would act illegally, ignoring the laws of the country that Texas had so adamantly wanted to join. After crossing into Comanche territory, the Rangers followed them to their primary camp at Little Robe Creek. There, they killed eighty Comanche, losing only one Ranger during the fight.

At first, this further convinced Texas that the Rangers knew how best to protect the Texans. It was the Rangers who were willing to go into enemy territory to ensure that the Native Americans weren't a problem, even if it made them the aggressors. In theory, the US was against invading other nations, though they had a very bad track record for recognizing the native peoples as nations.

As the people extolled the Rangers' methods in protecting them, the Rangers began to change. For two decades, the people of Texas would learn that this new, aggressive approach was not the boon that they had first thought. Without another enemy to fight, the Rangers would soon turn their attention to people who they suspected of being criminals.

Official Approval of the Agency and a New Wave of Problems

The Texas Rangers had been established when Texas was a nation, but they required new approval under the US government. In 1874, the Texas Rangers were first approved by the Texas Legislature to act on behalf of the new state. Working with the US Army, they finally succeeded in entirely removing both the Comanche and Kiowa from Texas.

There were many problems with the removal of an entire population of people, but one of the biggest issues for the Americans was that it removed any distraction the Rangers had. Just as there had been an influx of settlers after Texas gained its independence from Mexico, the removal of the native population from the region attracted the attention of other potential settlers. Soon there was another large wave of settlers coming into the region. While Texas was spacious, there were not limitless resources and lands. Much of the state is still too harsh a climate for settlers to thrive. This was not as widely known among the new settlers at the time, and they expected to find a safe, fertile land where they could prosper. After all, the nation had just fought a war to acquire it. Surely this would not have occurred if the lands were largely barren. As they arrived and realized that the habitable areas were far more limited, people began to fight over the lands.

In 1877, open fighting occurred around the salt lakes located close to today's San Elizario. The Rangers had little else to occupy their time, and to earn their pay, they had to take their job seriously. Unfortunately for the settlers, the Rangers had learned to be aggressive, not rational. They would soon put these practices to use against the settlers, who were suddenly far less enthusiastic of the tactics that they had applauded against the Comanche and other native tribes. There would be a number of clashes throughout Texas, with the Fence Cutting Wars of the 1880s being among the most interesting, which is described in greater detail in the next chapter.

They did help to fight against the Conner gang, a criminal family who terrorized Sabine County. They lived in what was called Deep East Texas. The Rangers were called in to handle the criminal family, which included a father and seven sons.

Originally, the Conners lived in Florida, but the promise of a new life in Texas drew them out, along with a lot of other families. They had left their home state of Florida in the hope of having a place where they could live, possibly without paying for anything. They were actually productive hog farmers for most of their years in Texas. The family thought that they owned all of the land around them, which proved not to be the case as they had not actually purchased the lands in Texas. Once someone else purchased the land, the family killed them. Two of the sons received prison time, and the father was still waiting for his trial to occur. However, before the trial could happen, the rest of their family broke them out of their cells, and the family went on the run. With eight men, they were a formidable force who were able to take on the lawmen that came after them. It is said that the family had come across one sheriff while hiding from the law. When he knew that he stood no chance, the sheriff told the family that for sparing his life, he would resign. When they let him go, the sheriff did quit, but he also let people know why.

The people in the region where the Conners were hiding found themselves the targets of nightly attacks. To take out the threat, the sheriff of the county asked for the Rangers to come and remove the problem. The Rangers decided the best way to learn about the family was to send lawmen to monitor the Conners and figure out where their hideout was. It was the law enforcement of the area who actually tailed the Conners. Upon learning where the family was hiding, the lawmen reported back to the Rangers. The leader of the Rangers then split his forces up into two groups and planned to attack just before sunrise. The Conners were apparently ready for them, though, and they managed to kill and injure several Rangers but lost three of their own. The rest of the Conners got away from the Rangers, continuing to fire on those who followed them.

With the Conners on the run, everyone who was in their path was at risk of being killed. The citizens began to form a posse because the Rangers were focused more on pursuit than protecting the people.

While the actions of the Conners were certainly extreme, the Rangers never seemed to try to talk to them. Their focus on pursuit over protection began to make the citizens uncomfortable at the very least and question the need for the Rangers at worst. The Rangers had not changed their aggressive approach, but chasing Americans through settlements was not the same as chasing Native Americans back to their homes. The citizens had not cared about the horrors perpetrated by the Rangers when it was against people they considered to be enemies, but having the Rangers be so aggressive with their neighbors was surprising. It eroded support for the

Rangers, and different towns would begin to create their own law enforcement. This would reduce the role that the Rangers would have within Texas. They were too violent and gained a reputation for shooting first and asking questions later. Local lawmen were seen as a better solution because they were more likely to try to talk with criminals first. By the beginning of the 20th century, citizens began to question whether the Texas Rangers were necessary.

Chapter 8 – The Fence Cutting Wars

Not all of the problems that the Texas Rangers dealt with were related to outside forces. The settlers also had problems with their neighbors, with the most notable internal feud being called the Fence Cutting Wars. Today, the name sounds comical, but it was a topic of extreme contention as the settlers were trying to carve out their own place in the new country. The introduction of barbed wire in the Wild West would create a reason for citizens to turn on each other, particularly as they had less concern about Native Americans or Mexicans attacking.

The Introduction of Barbed Wire

Prior to the introduction of barbed wire, it was incredibly difficult for ranchers and farmers to keep roaming animals and other ranchers off of their land. The large, unfenced areas could end up costing settlers their profits, as there was no way to stop theft without having constant guards, which was ineffective at best. It came to a point where ranchers and farmers had to work on areas of their land that they could more easily maintain. Considering many of them had purchased over four thousand acres, that meant that they were putting only a fraction of their lands to use.

The introduction of barbed wire in the Wild West made it easier for ranchers and farmers to mark their lands and deter animals and people from entering. The man given credit for the invention of the wire fence is Michael Kelly. His fences included a single strand of wire, though initially, the fences were not barbed. The weight of cows made this a very ineffective fence, as they could easily break through it and leave the area where they were meant to graze. Realizing that it was not adequate enough for its intended use, Kelly reinforced the fence by twisting two wires together, similar to a cable. This came to be known as the "thorny fence" because barbs were added to the two wires as a deterrent to the cows. This proved to be far more effective as the cows tended to keep their distance from the barbs.

As more people moved west, people sought to improve Kelly's design, some for their own farms, but many so that they could profit from successful patents. The man best known for improving Kelly's thorny fence was Joseph Glidden. As a farmer who lived in De Kalb, Illinois, Glidden had a personal stake in having an effective wire fence, though he also made sure to have his product patented, as seen by the moniker, the "King of the Barb." He won a patent in 1874 because he provided a simple wire barb that was woven into a double-strand wire. This not only reinforced the wire, but it also ensured that the barbs would remain in place as long as the wire held. In addition to making a durable fence, Glidden invented a way to mass-produce the fencing. His design is the one that is best known today.

The Problems with Texan Lands

Much of Texas in the 19th century was wild, open grasslands. It had very few natural barriers with which to mark territories, with even rocks and timber being uncommon. This meant it was difficult to know where one person's land ended and another's began. Trying to install fences meant doing it all from scratch, leaving room for error in placement and the potential for feuds over land claims. Having to erect a fence without trees or rocks almost always meant that the entire fence would need to be installed, which could be very costly. The fences were not very effective either.

The attempt to secure lands began with very basic forms of barbed wire as far back as 1857. The introduction of Kelly's barbed wire would create a boom in sales for those who could afford it. Mass production made the material more readily available, and the open stretches of lands were the perfect place for the new product.

The problem with barbed wire was that not everyone could afford it. Without any kind of marker to indicate where boundaries were, people began to dispute the boundaries of their lands, particularly as barbed wire began to be put up on lands that were not well defined. Even more problematic, some people, like the XIT Ranch, put barbed wire up over roads and other places that were traveled by other citizens. Some people were even bold enough to fence in public areas. This kind of activity caused a lot of disputes, interrupted the delivery of mail, and made it harder to get to water and public access to grazing areas. The laws were meant to calm tensions, but they had the opposite effect, as law enforcement would come down much harder on people who cut fencing without warning landowners than on those people who violated the laws of blocking public areas.

With the drought of 1883, the problems with unregulated barbed wire fencing became impossible to ignore. People began to cut the wires, usually at night. While these people called themselves Blue Devils, Javelinas, and Owls, the citizens usually called them nippers. According to a *Galveston News* report, nippers had destroyed more than seven hundred acres worth of property near Waco alone. Other reports have nippers causing about twenty million dollars in damages, and their activities also resulted in three deaths.

Many Texas politicians were not willing to actively speak out against the nippers, though. Although what they were doing could be considered illegal, a lot of fencing was also illegal. The nippers were attempting to ensure that water was not monopolized by a few people, particularly during the drought. Laws were passed in 1884 that made wire cutting illegal, but a lot of Texans did not agree with the laws, particularly since the laws had been passed more to protect wealthy and large farms. The laws did make it illegal to fence in public lands and roads unless a gate was included so that people could pass through it. While offenders were given six months to comply, many of them did not bother to fix their fencing.

The Rangers Become Involved

When it became clear that the laws were being largely ignored in Navarro County, the Texas Rangers were called in to handle the problem. Two Rangers became the primary leads in resolving the problem, Sergeant Ira Aten and Private Jim King. Their approach was different from what many of the other Rangers had done. Since citizens were acting at night and were armed, the two men decided the best approach was to blend in with the citizens. They took jobs working in the cotton fields, learning what they needed to know about the nighttime activities of possible nippers.

When they began to learn who the nippers in the area were, they chose a much more extreme method of handling the problem. Neither men paid attention to the ranchers who were not complying with the laws that stated not to block roads or public lands. The Rangers only moved against people who were trying to ensure that everyone had a chance to access water. Perhaps since they would be outnumbered, the two Rangers decided to place dynamite along some of the fencing. When the nippers cut those areas, there was an explosion, which was clearly an extreme solution that was not welcomed by the people in the area.

The adjutant general quickly spoke out against these extreme actions by the Rangers and ordered that they stop using dynamite to deter nipping. The damage was already done, though. While the nippers were largely stopped, and the Fence Cutting Wars slowed, then stopped, this kind of method used against citizens made the people view the Texas Rangers in a much dimmer light, preferring their own law enforcement over the aggressive, extreme actions of the Rangers.

Chapter 9 – The Injustice Perpetrated by the Texas Rangers

Every law enforcement agency has a dark chapter in its history, and that includes the Texas Rangers. Often, they are portrayed as the good guys or as victims of the villains in movies and TV. However, this group of law enforcement agents has a record of ignoring the law when dealing with minority groups, particularly Mexicans and Native Americans.

Discriminatory Practices

The Texas Rangers were formed to fight the Native Americans along the borders of Texas. The way that they treated Native Americans over the history of the organization helped to form the way they would look at other nations and races. Since they were originally given the roles of judge, jury, and executioner, the Rangers often killed native peoples instead of trying to resolve things peacefully. What is perhaps more concerning is that some Native Americans were a part of the early Texas Rangers, serving more as a way of dissuading other natives from attacking, as well as to track criminals.

The majority of Texans seemed perfectly fine to let the Texas Rangers do whatever the Rangers thought was best. The problems that began to emerge with the Texas citizens toward the end of the 19th century had always been a problem in other communities, particularly the Native American and Mexican communities. Citizens largely didn't care because those actions had not affected them, so it was considered to be normal. That was until the problems began to affect them, and the citizens learned firsthand just how brutal the Rangers could be. However, Native Americans, Mexicans, and African Americans already knew how violent and dangerous the Rangers had the potential to be.

The discrimination and persecution of entire groups of people would only get worse until it was finally addressed in the first half of the 20th century. However, it would get much worse before it got better.

Anti-Hispanic Sentiment

Following the end of the Mexican-American War, the Texas Rangers seemed to embody the American ideal that they were superior to their Mexican neighbors. This resulted in a policy of intolerance and violence that still mars the reputation of the organization. Many executions, lynchings, and other acts of violence were perpetrated against Hispanics after the end of the war. The killings and violence would reach a crescendo in the early part of the 20th century.

It is estimated that three hundred Mexicans were murdered by the Texas Rangers or by mobs led by the organization between 1915 and 1916. The violence occurred in large part because two Texas governors used the group more as goons than as a form of law enforcement. Both Governor James Ferguson and Governor William Hobby espoused anti-Hispanic rhetoric that exacerbated public opinion and the call to violence. Words alone would not have the desired effect, so to further dissuade Mexicans from immigrating into Texas, the Texas Rangers acted more like thugs who intimidated Mexicans, as well as African Americans.

When Mexican men were not willing to sell their lands, the governors would send the Texas Rangers to try to persuade them. When that didn't work, they killed the men to try to persuade their wives to sell the land to the government. The Rangers were not the only ones to perpetrate disturbing acts of intimidation and murder, but the fact that they had the state's consent to act so shamefully emboldened some of the worst of them. The kinds of Rangers who had been popular among the people had left after the war because the agency had not been required. They moved on to play major, as well as minor, roles within the US government, leaving behind a lot of people who were less capable and preferred to have power than to act in good conscience. As the remaining Rangers became more like thugs and criminals, their illegal conduct was covered up by the governors who approved of what they were doing.

Under Texas House Representative Claude Hudspeth, the Rangers would be used as a way of stirring up xenophobia against the Mexicans. Claiming that the borders were not strong enough, Hudspeth tried to convince the people of the United States that Mexicans posed a threat to the Americans prospering along the border. Where there was once relatively free movement and more friendly relations between Mexico and the US, Texas began to pass laws that forced a strict boundary that was meant to prevent political and social interaction, as well as limit immigration. Mexicans were killed when they owned land in Texas, leaving the survivors to largely act as laborers in lands that once belonged to Mexico.

The kinds of horrors that the Rangers perpetrated against the Native Americans largely ended when the Rangers drove the native peoples off their own land. However, the Rangers continued to kill Mexicans along the border without any justification. The book *The Injustice Never Leaves You* takes a harder look at the persecution

Mexicans faced in Texas until the Rangers were finally forced to stop.

Former Slaves

Texas was among the southern states that seceded from the US during the American Civil War, and they treated their slaves just as badly as the rest of the southern states. Like Native Americans, the people who would become to be known as African Americans were persecuted long before Texas became independent. As discussed above, slaves were brought to Texas with the original American settlers, despite the fact that the laws barred it. Special allowances were made and were then exploited as American settlers decided not to recognize the requirements that Spain and then Mexico made regarding slaves. Slaves were supposed to be able to purchase their freedom, something that the American settlers did not like and largely ignored. They were also less than pleased with the fact that former slaves were able to earn a higher status in society (though always below people of European descent) and to buy their own land. American settlers would further be angered when Mexico would say that slavery would be outlawed entirely over time.

The threat of eventually having to pay their slaves was one of the major reasons why Texas fought for its independence from Mexico. Once it was independent, Texas sought to perpetuate the system that would soon drive the US into the American Civil War. Had they known that the US would not continue to be a nation that supported slavery, it is likely that the institution would have continued in Texas long after it was outlawed in the US. During the Civil War, many people moved to regions farther from where Union troops were stationed in an effort to keep their slaves from revolting or trying to join the Union soldiers. Of course, it was futile, and Texas would be forced to give up slavery when the US beat the Confederates in 1865.

This did not mean that the Texans didn't try to retain the lifestyle for as long as possible. Given how large the state was, they continued to keep their slaves working without pay until they were found out, and in some cases, it would be a few years before their illegal actions were discovered and punished. Slave owners were no longer united, though, so each individual who refused to comply were eventually discovered and stopped.

Feeling that they were being persecuted for their belief that African Americans were not people or were lesser people, Texans began to make codes that were meant to keep their former slaves from integrating with society. One of the reasons that Texas was so quick to enact laws oppressing African Americans was due to the election of nine African Americans as state delegates. Fearing that their former slaves would become equal, or perhaps as harsh and cruel as the slaveholders had been, Texas began to pass laws that ensured that African Americans would not be able to vote.

This kind of illegal manipulation of the legal system would not be stopped until the latter half of the 20th century. However, for several decades, the Rangers treated African Americans terribly. They were not as actively violent against African Americans as they were against Mexicans, as they largely left the persecution of African Americans to the Texas Legislature.

Part II – Famous Texas Rangers and Their Most Famous Standoffs

Chapter 10 – Some of the More Notable Texas Rangers

With more than 150 years largely working for the benefit of Americans, the Texas Rangers have produced some admirable men. Their names may not be known among the general American populace, but they have gained recognition among many of the people in Texas. As seen in the following chapter, some of the criminals that the Texas Rangers faced were among the most notorious in American history.

John Coffee Hays

The first famous member of the Texas Rangers, John Coffee Hays, served the organization during one of its most difficult times. The Texas Revolution had freed the people of Texas from the perceived injustices of Santa Anna and Mexico, but it also left them incredibly vulnerable to attacks from enemies. Amidst the influx of settlers and confusion, Hays became a well-respected Ranger, entering the annals of Texas history as the first famous member of the organization.

Hays fought in both the Texas Revolution and the Mexican-American War, and he was instrumental in both of them. It was through his work and prowess in tracking and scouting that the Rangers began to be recognized as a reliable and competent agency. His ability to lead went beyond what many of the soldiers had expected, especially as it was the first time many of the soldiers had gone to war.

The reputation that the Texas Rangers have enjoyed today is largely because of Hays's abilities to take on the guerrilla fighters. However, he did not remain long after the Mexican-American War ended. Having earned his reputation in Texas, he moved west to the region that would soon become the state of California. Hays moved on from law enforcement to politics and was one of the founders of today's city of Oakland. During his time as a Ranger, he likely knew what kinds of problems to expect as a rancher, something he did in California.

Samuel Walker

One of the early members of the Rangers under Hays, Samuel Walker, had one of his first major offenses against the Comanche during the Battle of Walker's Creek. Walker was among the few who were injured in the battle, but upon his recovery, he quickly earned a name for himself. By the start of the Mexican-American War, he would be the second most notable Ranger, after John Hays.

One of the reasons that the Rangers had been successful in quickly defeating the Native Americans was the introduction of the Colt revolver, which is considered to be one of the first practical revolvers. As the Americans fought the Mexican-American War, Walker would look at the design of the Colt and determine several ways in which it could be improved. His new version of the weapon made it the deadliest firearm of the war. It would be his biggest contribution to the Rangers. Walker died during the Battle of Huamantla in early October 1847.

Ben McCulloch

Even if he had not made a name for himself, Ben McCulloch was the neighbor to one of the most famous people of the time, Davy Crockett. It was following Crockett that led McCulloch to Texas in 1835. The reason that McCulloch wasn't at the Alamo when it fell was because he was suffering from measles. By the time he recovered, the Alamo had already been lost. Wanting revenge, he joined Sam Houston to fight at the Battle of San Jacinto, and he then joined the Rangers at the Battle of Plum Creek. He earned a position as Hays's first lieutenant before the war with Mexico. General Zachary Taylor also employed McCulloch as his chief scout.

Like Hays, McCulloch headed toward California to try to earn his fortune. However, when the Civil War broke out, he was already back in Texas. In 1861, he was promoted to the position of Confederate brigadier general. He died fighting for the losing side at the Battle of Pea Ridge in 1862.

William Wallace – Bigfoot

William Wallace was a large man, reaching the height of six feet tall and a weight of 240 pounds before he was even twenty years old. This earned him the nickname of Bigfoot back in his hometown of Lexington, Kentucky. Having learned that his brother had been killed in the Goliad massacre, Wallace headed to Texas in 1836, planning to get revenge. However, he was too late to fight in the war, but he still remained in Texas, taking up residence in San Antonio.

Wallace finally got a chance to get revenge for his brother's death in 1842 when Mexico invaded. Unfortunately, Wallace ended up being taken prisoner and remained as one for two years. He spent that time in one of the most notorious Mexican prisons located in Veracruz.

By the time he got out, Wallace had decided to join the Rangers. Serving under Hays, Wallace would gain a reputation as a capable

Ranger and leader. By the 1850s, he had been put in charge of his own company.

He was one of the most notable members of the Rangers who were against secession. He did not leave the state, though. Despite this, he did fight against Union soldiers, though he also sought to protect the frontiers from other attacks. Wallace managed to survive the war, and he would gain a reputation as a great storyteller. Because of this, he would become one of the first folk heroes of the state, with his tales of fighting in the Wild West being far more novel when he died in 1899—he managed to live long enough to see the sharp decline of the Wild West into a place that was more subdued and law-abiding, something he helped to bring about.

John B. Armstrong

John B. Armstrong grew up in Tennessee, but he did not get along with the Reconstruction-era representatives following the end of the Civil War. Instead of continuing to fight, Armstrong moved to Texas, where there were far fewer authorities from the Union side, when he was 22 years old.

The reason Armstrong is still a notable member of the Rangers was because of his work in finally taking down the infamous John Wesley Hardin in 1877, a man who is covered in a later chapter. One of the reasons that Armstrong gained his reputation was that he was wounded from a gunshot wound when he requested to be put on the Hardin case, then tracked the criminal all the way to Florida. Armstrong also managed to do something that likely seemed impossible—he took the famous gunslinger alive so that Hardin had to go to trial for murder.

John B. Jones

It was John B. Jones who helped to establish the Rangers as a notable law enforcement agency after the end of the Civil War. He had distinguished himself during the Civil War, so he knew how chaotic things could be without the law. He and his forces managed to preserve the law during a time that is well remembered for hectic and dangerous situations.

Jones also took down one of the most notable criminals in the history of Texas, Sam Bass, who is covered in the next chapter. Unlike Armstrong, Jones was not able to take Bass in alive. His capture, and subsequent death, was considered to be when the Wild West was finally tamed, and Bass's death was a critical time for the Texas Rangers. It became harder for them to continue to operate with the aggressive approach they had become famous for up to that point. Though Bass was feared, the general population loved him. He shared his wealth, which he stole from people who could afford it. The fact that the Rangers started by shooting at him (epitomizing the adage of shoot first, ask questions later) called into question their methods, something that would become more openly criticized over the years.

Captain Bill McDonald

Captain Bill McDonald would be one of the first Rangers near the top who would have to face how the Rangers were functioning, as they could not continue to operate the way they had since the agency's inception. McDonald was the most well-known Ranger of the time, so it was up to him to implement the changes that would finally see the organization stop practices that were no longer acceptable, such as the aggressive approach that the Rangers had become notorious for using. Serving as the captain of the Rangers from 1891 to 1907, he helped to go after high-profile criminals and problems of the state.

McDonald had the kind of attitude toward crime that you would expect of a Ranger—he was incredibly confident. To this time, he is attributed as having said. "One riot—one Ranger," a sentiment that he certainly lived by, even if he did not actually say it. One of the most notable examples of his bravado was during a prize fight that occurred in Dallas while he was the captain of the Rangers. He was there to break it up, but he came alone. When the community asked him when his backup would arrive, he is said to have replied, "Hell! Ain't I enough? There's only one prize fight!" McDonald still retained a lot of the confident attitude from the early days of the Rangers but was helping to transition the group into something that would continue in the new era. Following his time as one of the leaders in the Rangers, they became respectable and reliable, and it was in large part because of his efforts that they became the agency they are today.

Frank Hamer

Frank Hamer had spent most of his life coming and going from the Rangers, though he stayed in law enforcement during most of his life. He first joined the agency in 1906 and became a part of the regular border patrol. Years after leaving the agency, Hamer returned and finally took on a more senior role in 1922. He remained one of the leading figures as the Rangers became more adept at law enforcement, as well as becoming less aggressive. However, Hamer did have to help balance between law enforcers and aggressors, as an oil boom during this time saw the quick rise and fall of many towns. This meant that there was a lot of tension that required a quick mind to assess how to respond. Hamer retired in 1934.

Retirement clearly was not the same for him as most people, though, as Hamer made his extensive services available to the Rangers as a special investigator. It was after his retirement that Hamer would gain his fame as the man who brought down the infamous Bonnie Parker and Clyde Barrow.

Chapter 11 – Sam Bass

Perhaps the first famous outlaw that the Texas Rangers faced was Sam Bass. Though he was not the man that legend has made him out to be, he was still a dangerous outlaw who posed a real challenge to the newly formed lawmen of the Texas Rangers. Like many of the people who met their end against the Texas Rangers, Sam Bass was a popular figure. Today he is sometimes called "Robin Hood on a Fast Horse" or "Texas' Beloved Bandit" because of what he was said to have done with the money he stole.

The Early Life of One of the Early Western Outlaws

The famous outlaw was born in 1851 near Mitchell, Indiana. Little is known of his parents, as he and his sisters and brothers were orphaned when he was young. Their uncle took them in, adding several more children to his brood of nine. With so many mouths to feed, and due to living in a rural part of the US, the children did not attend school for formal education.

At the age of eighteen, Sam went out to earn his own living in Mississippi. During his first year in the state, he learned how to shoot and became an adept card player. His time in Mississippi was short as he soon befriended Scott Mayes. His new friend was heading to Denton, Texas, an idea that intrigued the young Sam Bass. Images of becoming a cowboy helped persuade Bass to leave with his friend.

Ironically, Sam's first known job was working with Sheriff W. F. Eagan, though not as a lawman. Sam had considerable experience on farms, so the sheriff employed him as a farmhand. During this time, Sam learned a great deal about the countryside and the roads because some of his work involved being a teamster. He would later use this knowledge to avoid capture.

Bass did live an honest life for several more years, earning a name for himself as a reliable, hardworking farmhand. With the money that he earned, he was able to save enough to buy an impressive mare to enter into horse races. Known as Denton Mare, the horse earned Sam more than enough money to stop working on Sheriff Eagan's farm and settle into a comfortable life of racing horses and gambling sometime in 1875. During this time, he would befriend several of the men who would eventually become his fellow outlaws. Bass turned to crime after he used his winnings to take a herd of cattle to sell in northern markets for more money. This part of the venture was successful. Where he failed was in turning to gold prospecting to try to gain even more money. By the time he and his business partner Joel Collins gave up, they were completely broke.

Instead of going back to work, the pair opted for robbing stagecoaches. Joining with two other men, they came to be known as the Black Hills Bandits, which was where they had moved as gold prospectors. Initially, they were very successful, holding up seven coaches in a matter of months. Realizing that the payoff their robberies brought would not be enough, the Black Hills Bandits moved on to much bigger targets.

Taking to Trains for Large Payout

Having decided that trains had far greater potential to set them up for life, the gang set up a date for their first train robbery, September

18th, 1877. They had six members by this point, so they were able to be more daring in their criminal activities. The plan was to strike at 10:48 p.m. and take control of Big Spring Station in Nebraska. With the station under their control, they had the next train stopped, and they boarded it.

They quickly learned, though, that the payoff was not quite as large as they had hoped. There was only $450 in the safe that was easy to access. The more secure safe was set on a timer and could not be opened until it reached a specific destination. Frustrated and not understanding how the safe couldn't be opened, the bandits ruthlessly beat the express messenger. Upset, they began to break other things on the train and were surprised to find several wooden boxes. In those boxes were gold pieces totaling $60,000. The riches were divided up, and the six men split up into pairs so that they would not all be caught at once. Two of them were killed within a week of the robbery. Another one of the pairs split up, with one half getting captured and the other likely escaping to Canada. Bass and a man named Jack Davis headed south.

During their trip south in a carriage, they encountered a group of detectives and soldiers who were looking for the six men who managed to pull off the train heist. With the money safely hidden under their seat, it was not obvious that they were two of the bandits. More surprising, they were successful in convincing the lawmen that they, too, were hunting the robbers for the reward. This worked, and after traveling together for four days, the lawmen and soldiers took a different way. No longer worried about being detected, Bass and Jack Davis headed to Denton, Texas. Here, Bass would enter into a new phase of his life. With his newfound wealth, which he explained was a mark of his success as a prospector, Bass drew a lot of attention. Not content to simply enjoy the wealth of $10,000, Bass would form his own gang and make robbing trains his new profession, at which he would be remarkably successful. It is also possible that he was not able to spend much of his money because they were in gold that had been minted by the US government. If this was the case, Bass likely hid most of his wealth. Whatever the case might have been, this new phase of his life proved to be much more exciting.

Exploiting a Weakened Texas and the Bass War

When Bass resettled in Texas in 1878, the state was recovering from their loss during the Civil War, like many of the southern states. Reconstruction had recently ended, but the state was large, and there were many who were hoping to manipulate the situation to become more powerful. In that way, they weren't too different from Sam Bass; it was just that they were trying to manipulate the system, while Bass was willing to blatantly break the law.

With the state in a much weaker condition than it had been since gaining its independence, the citizens of Texas wanted protection from bandits and gangs. The people seeking greater power began to promise to crack down on illegal activities, and they quickly called in the Texas Rangers.

Bass had earned himself a name for the successes he and his gang had achieved, which made him a target of politicians and would-be politicians, who decided to make an example of him and his gang. With the backing of so many, the Texas Rangers took the capture of Bass very seriously. Indeed, it became their primary focus.

Having learned all of the backroads and trails when he had lived in Texas working as a farmhand and teamster, Bass and his men were able to elude the Texas Rangers. The distinct advantage of knowing the terrain and areas made the Texas Rangers look like they were inept, which obviously upset the Rangers. They were not accustomed to fighting an advisory who knew the area better than they did, and they eventually realized they would have to find another tactic to finally capture the Bass Gang. Focusing on flushing out the people who were helping the bandits, the Rangers arrested Henderson Murphy and his son Jim. Faced with charges of stealing from the federal mail, Murphy agreed to rejoin the Bass Gang. As a member, Murphy would betray his former boss, not only to save his own hide but also with the hope of getting some of the large reward that had been placed on Bass's head.

Unaware that Murphy had turned on them, the gang went to his home to rest in April 1878. The Rangers found them there, and a shootout ensued. Bass was hit in his cartridge belt and on his rifle, suffering no injuries to his body. Still, it was a harrowing experience, and the gang initially headed north after the shooting. By June, they decided it would be safest to head south after a posse challenged them to a gunfight, in which one of the gang members died.

Sam Bass's Demise

Chasing the Bass Gang proved to be not only tricky but also dangerous, as a number of people across Texas tried to take down the outlaw themselves. Bass managed to kill a number of citizens who were hoping to score the reward for his death. One of these attempts resulted in the Rangers learning of his position. Ranger Ware had been nearby at the time, with legend saying that he interrupted the shave he was getting to pursue the gang. With the foam from the shave still on his face, Ware met Major Jones, who had also heard about the gunfight that resulted in the death of Deputy Grimes. Jones shot at Bass as he and the gang were heading to their horses, drawing attention to himself and Ware. Two citizens and Ranger Harold soon joined the two Rangers, and together they found the gang mounting their horses. Bass was seriously wounded during the encounter.

The evidence seems to support the claim that Ranger Ware had been the man to shoot the outlaw. According to the doctors of the time, the bullet had broken upon striking Bass's belt cartridge and entered in two places after the belt split. Bass also recounted that he had been hit before reaching the horses, saying that he was hit by a man with lather on his face. Ware himself did not claim to have been the successful shooter, making way for Harold to take credit. Bass had gained so much notoriety at the time that people feared retaliation for successfully hurting him or his men. This is likely why Ware was all right with Harold receiving credit for injuring Bass.

The survivors of the Bass Gang escaped, including Bass himself, but he would not be on the run for long. Afraid that there would be more people put at risk if they continued to pursue Bass, the Rangers backed off. They instead focused on tracking the Bass Gang. When they encountered a man propped up against a tree the next day, they initially ignored him under the belief that the man was a tired railroad worker. When the Rangers did eventually approach the man, he held up his hands and confessed who he was.

Finally in custody, Bass did not provide the Rangers with any helpful information that would help them capture the three remaining Bass Gang members. At the time, Bass said that he had not killed anyone unless it was due to his shots during the final shootout that resulted in the death of Deputy Grimes. This was an extraordinary admission, considering how notorious and dangerous he was considered to be at the time. He died the next day, July 21st, 1887.

This proved to be a boon for the Rangers, as the Texas Legislature was debating whether the agency was even necessary anymore. With the capture of Bass, they proved that they had a place and a purpose in the state.

This was not the only legacy from Bass's life and death, though. His reputation grew considerably after his death, which is a real feat considering how much fear his name inspired at the time. Cowhands came up with a song to sing to their cattle called "The Ballad of Sam Bass," which was created by John Denton, and it was used to soothe their charges on rough nights. Sam's fame continued to grow, and it got to the point where he was added to Madame Tussauds wax museums by the end of the 19th century.

Chapter 12 – John Wesley Hardin

When people talk about bad guys or Wild West men who wear black, there are few whose reputations rival that of John Wesley Hardin. It is thought that he shot and killed more than thirty men during his 42 years of life. Most of Hardin's life was spent on the run, though he periodically attempted to settle down on a few occasions. Ironically, he would be pardoned toward the end of his life and become a lawyer before getting himself killed because of a woman. Even if he wasn't the first outlaw (or even the most well-remembered), he put fear into the hearts of anyone who crossed him, except for the Texas Rangers and a few of the men he employed who were just as hard and potentially cruel as Hardin himself.

Early Life

Born to a Methodist preacher and his wife in 1853 in Bonham, Texas, John Wesley Hardin seemed to have everything he needed in life to succeed. Not only did his father have a steady job with the church, but he was also a lawyer, a professional combination that would seem to lend extra morality to his children. Instead, Hardin would show his violent tendencies fairly early in life. He was only fourteen years old when he stabbed one of his classmates. The next year, Hardin would commit his first murder, shooting an African American in Polk County. Soon the lawmen of Polk County were after him, setting Hardin down the path that would make him one of the most notorious Texan outlaws in American history.

When Hardin made his first kill, the American Civil War had just recently ended. Surrounded by those who had helped to put down the way of life that Texas had been trying to maintain since taking the land from Mexico, the people of Texas were being forced to acquiesce to the nation that had initially rejected them. Hardin's open aggression could have been a product of the unhealthy environment around him. The people of Texas were now being forced to view their slaves as people, and not everyone was willing to do that. The fact that the Union soldiers in the state would treat the killing of an African American as murder may have been unexpected.

A Trail of Blood

Looking at his violent history, it would seem that murder was only a matter of time for the young Hardin. Once he started down that path, he took to it like a fish in water. While fleeing from the lawmen, Hardin killed between one and four Union soldiers who were trailing him.

He would eventually become a cowboy who worked along the Chisolm Trail during 1871, which kept him constantly on the move. During that year, it is estimated that he killed seven more people. After this, he headed to Abilene, Kansas, where he added another three people to his growing list of victims. During his short stay in Abilene, he encountered the famous "Wild Bill" Hickok. When a couple of friends of Hardin got upset at Hickok for defacing an obscene image the outlaws had painted on the side of one of their buildings, those friends tried to push Hardin to fight Hickok. They told Hardin about Hickok's origins, constantly calling the famous Wild Bill a Yankee who hated rebels (the term for Southerners). Their ploy failed, though, as Hardin knew Wild Bill's reputation and respected him. However, Hardin and Hickok did end up coming face to face. When he was a lawman, Hickok told Hardin that he was wearing guns against the city's ordinance. Hardin initially seemed to comply, handing the pistols over, but he rotated them at the last moment so Hickok was looking down the barrels. Hardin did not do anything, though, and both men went their separate ways. Later that year, Hickok and Hardin were out on a cattle drive, and Hickok allowed Hardin to take his pistols back into town, something that Hardin would revel in because he was seen as having a close relationship with the famous gunfighter. Things would likely have played out very differently had Hickok been aware of who Hardin actually was. At the time, Hardin was going by an alias, so the people in the city did not know he was a wanted man.

Almost immediately after arriving in Texas, Hardin got into trouble with the state police. He was arrested for killing the Waco city marshal, though he claimed not to have been the perpetrator. The problem was soon resolved, leaving Hardin free to marry Jane Bowen. They would have three children, and for a while, he seemed to be trying to live a more settled life. However, it did not last long, and Hardin and his young family would spend a lot of the next few years on the run.

Captured by the Texas Rangers

The number of people that Hardin killed varies depending on the source, but it was known that he worked with anti-Reconstructionists against law enforcement. After killing former State Police Captain Jack Helm, then the deputy sheriff of Brown County, Hardin had to take his family to Florida in 1874. Unwilling to let the murderer get away, the Texas Rangers pursued him. Finally, in July of 1877, they finally caught up with the outlaw in Pensacola, Florida. At least one Ranger lost his life during the fight to capture Hardin.

Once in custody, Hardin was taken back to Texas to be tried. He was given 25 years in prison in September 1878, although he wouldn't even serve two decades before being pardoned in 1894. Most of the time that he had spent in prison was dedicated to following in his father's footsteps as a lawyer. Despite his crimes, Hardin joined the Texas bar not long after his pardon. However, he soon got into trouble because of an affair he had with one of his client's wives. When the husband found out, Hardin hired assassins to kill him. Apparently, Hardin didn't want to actually kill now that he was a notable pillar of the community of El Paso. Some say that he did not pay the assassin, though, which could have been one of the reasons for what happened next. On August 19th, 1895, John Selman, Sr. entered the Acme Saloon, where Hardin was carousing. Walking up to the man, Selman shot him in the head. Even though Hardin died after the first shot, Selman fired three more shots into Hardin after he slumped to the floor.

Hardin's life was largely defined by violence, but he was unique in that he largely acted like a gentleman when he wasn't killing. According to him, he never killed anyone who didn't deserve it, a claim that was obviously untrue considering he killed lawmen and people who had done him no wrong. Unlike Bass, Hardin was not considered a hero, and his death was not met with a similar backlash.

Chapter 13 – The Assassination Attempt

Four American presidents have been assassinated, but a far greater number have actually survived assassination attempts. The most famous assassination in Texas was the successful slaying of President John F. Kennedy. Less well known today, though, was the assassination attempt against President William Howard Taft. Taft himself would say that it was the Texas Rangers who saved his life.

A Historic Meeting

After the turn of the century, Mexico and the US were finally willing to talk and establish a healthier relationship. US President Taft and Mexican President Porfirio Díaz took the time to decide what would be the best way to meet and to discuss what they would need to do going forward. Up to this point, there had been no official relationship between the two neighboring countries, so there was a lot of potential in starting to heal the damage caused by the annexation of Texas and the Mexican-American War. After all, both nations had overthrown what they viewed as oppressive foreign nations. The United States and Mexico had far more in common and would stand to benefit by developing a good relationship.

The question was how to do that without bringing up past events and potentially offending the other leader. On both sides, there was opposition to the move because there were people who still held a grudge; it had only been half a century, and people on both sides continued to feel wronged.

In an effort to ensure neutrality, both presidents agreed that they would meet along the Chamizal strip, located between El Paso, Texas, and Ciudad Juárez, Chihuahua. No national flags would be flown in this region for the meeting. Unfortunately, making the location common knowledge meant that those who still held grudges knew exactly where the two leaders would be and when. Both sides knew that they were putting their leaders at greater risk by doing this, and they worked to minimize the danger to their lives. They deployed four thousand soldiers from both militaries, agents from both the FBI and Secret Service, and the US Marshals. An additional 250 Americans joined in the security detail in an effort to ensure that Taft would be safe. However, the men who knew the area best were the Texas Rangers, and it was their knowledge that would prove instrumental in ensuring that both presidents survived.

The Attempt on Two Presidents' Lives

The two men were to meet on October 16th, 1909, at the summit that was to finally change the relationship between the neighboring countries. Ranger Private C.R. Moore and Frederick Russell Burnham, the leader of the 250 private citizens, were going over the area to ensure that everything was ready. They encountered a man at El Paso's Chamber of Commerce, who was holding a concealed pistol. The building was located along the route that both presidents were already taking to hold the summit. The two men immediately apprehended the would-be-assassin shortly before the presidents came into the range of the man's pistol.

The summit was successful, but President Díaz was aging, and the Mexicans would rebel against him during 1910. According to the peace the two presidents had brokered, the US would not have any military interference in the country. Since Díaz was an authoritarian, he likely did not want to be displaced by the US and a puppet put in his place. When the Mexicans began to rise up against their president in 1910, the US stood to lose a lot of money as they had invested in the country, despite the strained relationship. The Mexican people began to riot against the close ties with the US, but the word was not passed on to Taft until a few months later. His reaction was to send soldiers to the border and the navy into the Gulf of Mexico. However, they were not to take any action without the express consent of Congress as it would be an act of war. The American military was not to do anything, no matter what they witnessed, to keep from starting an unauthorized war. The rioting did spill over into Arizona, with two citizens being killed. Despite the provocation, Taft was able to convey the need to remain out of the fighting. Though it was tense, another war was averted because of the success of the summit in October the previous year, which would have never been possible without the efforts of the Texas Rangers.

Chapter 14 – Role in the Bandit War

The name suggests that this was a war between bandits in Texas and that the Rangers had to break it up, but the truth is more complicated. The problem wasn't with outlaws but with members of the community who abused their power during the 1910s. The decade has come to be known as the Bandit War, Bandit Era, Time of the Bandit Trouble, and Era of Shame because it seemed almost hopeless that the state would ever fully remove the corruption. It was the uncontrolled methods of the Rangers, which were openly violent and racist,

that would eventually require the Rangers to be reined in, and it remains one of the greatest stains on their history. After this period, citizens would have little faith in the Texas Rangers, as they proved to be as corrupt as the criminals they were chasing. It would only be under a new leader in the 1920s that the reputation of the Rangers would begin to recover.

Rotten on the Inside

With the Civil War about half a century in the past, many of the southern states had recovered to some degree. However, corruption had taken hold in many of them, as racism had been institutionalized. At the time, Texas was the biggest state in the US, and it was still known for being largely part of the Wild West. This reputation was exacerbated by the widespread corruption and criminal activity that continued almost unchecked. From cattle rustlers and gangs to corrupt politicians, there were a lot of underhanded activities occurring across the Lone Star State. It got so bad that the Texas Rangers had to increase patrols along the Mexican/Texan border to prevent criminals from escaping across the border or returning if they were successful in fleeing the lawmen the first time around.

Some of the problems stemmed from the Mexican rebellion that started in 1910. The Texas governor hoped to stem some of the problems growing in Texas, particularly among people of Mexican descent, by appointing Henry Ransom to be the captain of the Texas Rangers in the southern part of the state. This appointment was made because Ransom had saved the life of a prominent army captain in the Philippines, Johan Hulen, who repaid Ransom by recommending him as a captain to the governor. Unfortunately, Ransom was a known killer, and resorting to violence was all too common with him. When Governor Ferguson commanded him to create a new Ranger company and "...go down there and clean it up— even if you have to kill every damn man connected with it [referring to the Plan of San Diego]," Ransom had no qualms with the direction. With a promise that he and his men would be immune from prosecution for murder, Ransom became exactly what the people had feared since the end of the previous century. There was no control over him, and he and his men operated more like bandits than lawmen.

The Plan of San Diego

Between 1915 and 1917, there were frequent outbursts of violence along the border. The more one side attacked, raided, and destroyed land on the other side, the more the other side would retaliate.

In the small Texas town of San Diego (not to be confused with San Diego, California), a group of Mexican supporters documented their plan to cause a revolution in the US that would see parts of Texas become another independent country. They hoped to win over other minorities by offering lands to the Native Americans and having the states be run by African Americans. It would have included more lands than just Texas.

The attacks were largely carried out around the lower regions of the Rio Grande Valley. Irrigation systems were destroyed, railroad trestles were damaged, and people were attacked. Americans in the area began to fear that the rise of racist propaganda would result in the slaughter of all of the Anglo-Americans. This was why Texas Governor Ferguson was so careless in his instructions to Ransom, fueling the fire instead of reducing the risks to the people.

The Bandit War Begins

Despite the fear inspired by the blatant violence against Anglo-Americans, many of them did not share the same opinion of how to resolve the problem as Ferguson. They wanted peace to be restored through legal means, which was certainly not what happened.

When reports came in of about fifty Mexicans crossing over the Rio Grande close to Brownsville in August 1915, Texas Ranger Captain Fox mobilized his men to the region. The day that they arrived, the Mexican rebel Luis de la Rosa attacked a small group of people in Sebastian, Texas. This was followed by looting and an announcement that he planned to kill prominent people in south Texas. As the *Dallas Morning News* pointed out, this declaration proved that it wasn't Mexico behind the attacks but a gang that was doing whatever they wanted to do.

So, citizens began to fight back, shooting people they believed to be bandits without any evidence. It was only after killing three suspects that the posse began to realize that they had killed innocent men.

Once the Rangers arrived, things initially got worse because they formed another posse that included Ransom. The posse had fourteen Rangers and eight men from the 12th Cavalry. They headed to the biggest ranch in Texas, the King Ranch. The posse grew as it moved, with the men feeling more excited about the upcoming fight.

Some of the men stopped at Norias Ranch, where they waited while the others went out to search for the raiders. One of the remaining leaders of the posse, Customs Inspector Hines saw men on the horizon and initially thought that they were the posse returning. However, he quickly realized they were wearing Mexican sombreros and assumed they were bandits. He notified the others, and they scattered in an attempt to get into defensive positions.

All of the approaching men were commanded by de la Rosa, though some were Mexican and others were a part of the Plan of San Diego. Their goal was to disrupt the train service and rob the train that would arrive there. Not expecting that there would be members of a posse, the rebels were not prepared for the initial attack. However, the raiders had roughly sixty men, and they quickly began a more aggressive attack once the shock was over.

It was the largest battle of the war, and it lasted for more than two hours as the sides picked off each other's members. De la Rosa was killed toward the end, and the raiders seemed to lose their desire to fight after that. They had expected an easy raid but had instead encountered a much larger contingent of well-armed defenders.

About an hour after the raid ended, the posse returned to Norias Ranch. All of the Rangers had missed the action, which upset many of them who wanted to engage in a gunfight. When Ransom began to criticize how the defenders had responded, Pinkie Taylor, a former Ranger, quickly cut off the spectator's criticism. Criticizing those who had just been under the assault of a large contingent of bandits would not be allowed, especially by a man who had just been made a Ranger.

Despite their desire to fight, the Rangers and other members of the posse decided not to chase the raiders that day. Waiting until the next day, they set off to follow the bandits. They found several dead rebels on the way, as well as one survivor. The survivor told them that the main drive behind the attack was to restore the Rio Grande Valley to Mexico. He died soon after, succumbing to the wounds he had sustained the previous day, though some think that Ransom may have killed him.

When a photographer arrived the next day to take pictures, the Rangers were more than happy to pose and take credit for what happened, even though they had not been a part of the fight. They treated the bodies of the bandits with contempt, dragging them behind their horses. This angered not only the Mexicans but also many Americans who saw the images.

Despite the anger on how the bodies were treated, people began to fear what was happening, and soldiers were sent to guard the border. Less than two weeks after the fight at the ranch, ten people had been killed without any evidence that they were a part of the plot. Citizens even started to shoot people who looked like armed Mexicans. Even after it was reported that the insurgents had all been captured and killed, the Rangers continued to pursue and kill people they suspected of being a part of the plan.

Initially, the plan had been to kill prominent citizens, but it soon became more of a rallying cry to raid and plunder areas. The response by the Rangers really wasn't any better. They killed innocent civilians under the guise of justice and did not face any consequences for killing innocent Mexicans. It created a sense of mistrust between Americans, Mexicans, and Mexican-Americans that still has not healed today.

Chapter 15 – Taking Down Bonnie and Clyde

Easily the two most well-known criminals that the Texas Rangers brought to justice were the infamous duo Clyde Champion Barrow and Bonnie Elizabeth Parker—better known simply as Bonnie and Clyde. Many people thought of them as heroes, similar to Sam Bass. Bonnie and Clyde were fighting the establishment that had prospered on the backs of Americans, or at least that is how many people saw them at the time. It was the restraint that the Rangers used, ensuring that no civilians were injured, that showed they had changed since the Bandit War.

The Barrow Gang

The famous couple met in January of 1930 when Bonnie was 19 and Clyde was 21. Bonnie was married when they met, but her husband was in prison for murder. Soon after their meeting, Clyde was arrested for stealing, but he escaped after Bonnie managed to get a gun to him. He was quickly recaptured and would finally be released in 1932. Bonnie was apparently waiting for him, and they began their infamous life of crime in Texas.

They were joined by other people soon after, including Raymond Hamilton, although he only did so for a few months. After he went his own way, William Daniel Jones joined the couple. When Ivan Barrow was released from prison in 1933, he joined his brother and Bonnie. His wife, Blanche, also joined the gang, bringing the total number of members to five (three men and two women). This was the start of the Barrow Gang. They quickly escalated their crimes, and their reputation grew beyond just Texas, capturing the attention of the entire country. The more they were able to elude the law, the more intense the hunt to capture them became. During their time together, the press and citizens usually called them the Barrow Gang or Barrow and Parker. The commonly known moniker Bonnie and Clyde was occasionally used, but it wasn't until the highly inaccurate movie *Bonnie and Clyde*, which was released in 1967, that the name was popularized. It seems that it was Bonnie who actually referred to them as Bonnie and Clyde, as she wrote the poem "The Story of Bonnie and Clyde." The poem was published in one of the Dallas papers around the time she died.

One of the reasons they were so adept at avoiding apprehension was that they were constantly on the move. Clyde knew many of the backroads, and he drove far faster than most law enforcement agents anticipated. He had also managed to steal a number of high-powered rifles from one of the National Guard armories, and he was not afraid to use them any more than the sawed-off shotguns and pistols he had. Considering he was somewhat paranoid and prone to shooting if he felt something was out of place, Clyde was a very dangerous man to approach. His firepower was superior to what most law enforcement had, making it less likely that anyone would try to take him alive. On the few occasions where he was trapped, Clyde was able to shoot his way out because of how many weapons he had.

In July 1933, Clyde's brother Ivan was killed in a shootout while the gang was in Iowa. His wife was taken by law enforcement. Jones was captured later that year in Houston.

Bonnie and Clyde managed on their own for a while, even escaping a trap set for them around Grand Prairie, Texas. After surviving the set-up, the couple stole the car of an attorney and drove to Oklahoma. Once they had put a lot of distance between themselves and the men who had nearly killed them, the couple abandoned the car. About a month later, they reached Louisiana, where they continued to steal from prominent people.

In January 1934, the pair was looking to rebuild their gang. Clyde opted to help five men escape from Eastham State Prison Farm, located in Waldo, Texas. The escaping prisoners used automatic pistols to shoot two guards. Once they were close to him, Barrow protected the fleeing prisoners by using a machine gun. Two notable escapees were the aforementioned Raymond Hamilton, who had been given a sentence in excess of two hundred years, and Henry Methvin.

A few months later, Bonnie and Clyde encountered two patrolmen in Grapevine, Texas. The two men were young and inexperienced, and before they had a chance to get their guns, the couple shot them. A few days later, they managed to abduct a police chief in Oklahoma and kill a constable.

Most of the crimes they committed were done in small places that were harder to find, making it easier for the gang to escape. The Rangers realized that they were visiting family, some who lived near Dallas, so the Rangers staked out near their homes. On a couple of occasions, they ended up in shootouts with law enforcement because they kept returning to their families.

It is interesting to note how close the pair was with their families, particularly as their families would spend decades insisting that Bonnie and Clyde only killed in self-defense. According to their surviving family, it was the other gang members who committed most of the killings for which the pair were blamed.

Backed by the FBI

By 1934, the couple was not only being chased by local and state law enforcement, but they had also become targets of the FBI. This agency was able to provide much more robust information on the pair and posted wanted notices around the country. They provided photographs of the couple, fingerprints, and data about them to law enforcement agencies around the nation as well. As Bonnie and Clyde had driven a stolen car to Louisiana, their crimes became a federal offense. With their record, the FBI immediately treated them as a serious threat.

The FBI placed most of its emphasis on tracking the couple in Louisiana. By April 1934, the FBI thought they had tracked the infamous duo to a remote location in the state near where the Methvins lived. While they wanted to capture some of the escaped convicts, their focus was on apprehending the two heads of the gang. Learning that the couple had thrown a party with Methvin and his family at one of the nearby lakes, the lawmen prepared to ambush the couple on their way back from the party as they headed to Sailes, Louisiana.

A small posse of FBI agents and Texas Rangers hid among the bushes beside the highway. Former Texas Ranger Frank Hamer was one of the men who were prepared to shoot upon seeing the couple's car. He had resigned in 1932 following the election of Governor Miriam Ferguson, whom he thought was too soft on crime. Considering his wealth of knowledge, Hamer made his services available as a special investigator. Louisiana hired him as a highway patrolman specifically to take down Bonnie and Clyde. He had become well acquainted with the kinds of patterns that Clyde tended to use when sticking to backroads, so Hamer was able to anticipate where the criminal duo was likely to go and the route they would use. Most of the credit for setting up the ambush goes to Sheriff Henderson Jordan of Louisiana because he was the one who had established an agreement to spare Methvin if the family would give up the couple. Without his persuasion with the Methvin family, law enforcement agents wouldn't have known where Bonnie and Clyde were. Hamer was also supposed to have a role in ensuring that Methvin was given immunity in Texas. Together, Hamer and Jordan were the two primary members of the posse who ensured that they were able to set up an ambush to finally stop the crime spree of the Barrow Gang. Without Bonnie and Clyde, they knew that the gang would disband.

The lawmen had made an attempt to catch the pair a few weeks before the ambush but had just missed them. The ambush was set up this time to ensure that this problem did not happen again. Hiding in brush and tall grass, the men waited for the couple to get within range.

Deputy Sheriff Oakley was the first to shoot at the infamous couple, ordering them to stop. Clyde was going at high speed and ignored the order. The duo had made it through similar ambushes before unscathed, and Clyde most likely figured that they would be able to escape again. As he neared them, Barrow managed to open one of the doors and seemed to ready himself to aim a sawed-off shotgun at the lawmen, but he was finally outmatched. With five officers quickly emerging from the grasses, he didn't have a chance to fire before the law enforcement agents began shooting. The car continued for roughly half a block before going into an embankment, as one of the lawmen had intentionally shot out a tire. Most of the rest of the shots had gone into the body of the car.

Six men had laid in wait to ambush Bonnie and Clyde. There was no shootout at the end because Clyde did not have a chance to fire by the time he realized the police were there. After six months of tracking them, Hamer perhaps describes the event best:

I can tell you what happened this morning. We just shot the devil out of them, that's all. That's all there was to it. We just laid a trap for them. A steel trap...We were hiding beside the road. All six of us on one side—we didn't want any cross-fire—and when they came along, we hollered at them to stop. They both reached for their guns, but they were kind of slow. Seemed like they must have had cramps or something.

They were too slow. They didn't get to fire a shot. The car smashed into an embankment after we fired. Clyde was driving when we tried to stop them. Bonnie was sitting beside him.

The reputation that the Barrow Gang earned as heroes of the people isn't entirely accurate, yet their deaths were not welcome to most people. However, the people who were aware of how dangerous the gang was were happy that they were finally stopped. With many of their early thefts being in shops and little out-of-the-way places, Bonnie and Clyde had killed civilians, as well as stolen from less wealthy people.

Whatever people felt for Bonnie and Clyde, their death was huge news that gained a lot of attention for Hamer. The interview that Hamer gave following the death of the couple was one of the few times he spoke of it to the media. He even turned down an invitation to celebrate being a national hero in Austin. He had no desire for the attention that the event shone on him—he simply wanted to stop the deadly criminals before they could kill anyone else.

Chapter 16 – The Murder of Irene Garza

Following the changes to the Rangers in the 1920s, the law enforcement organization acted much more like lawmen than outlaws. The fact that they produced someone who was able to calculate how best to approach the notorious Bonnie and Clyde, and prevent any civilians from being harmed shows how far they had come since the 1910s. By the 1960s, the Texas Rangers had evolved into a reliable and reputable law enforcement agency that was dedicated to ensuring that justice was served.

One of the most intriguing cases of the Texas Rangers in the 1960s was the death of Irene Garza. It would take more than half a century to finally solve the murder, but the Rangers did manage to bring her killer in.

The Murder

Irene Garza had lived in McAllen, Texas. She had grown up in the state, becoming the first Latina twirler at McAllen High School, then became the first member of her family to graduate from college. During her time in college, she had become both the homecoming and prom queen, and she was given the crown of Miss All South

Texas Sweetheart in 1958. After all of these accomplishments, Garza settled down in McAllen, Texas, and became a schoolteacher for the poorer children in the town.

In April of 1960, she had taken the family car to go to church. As a good Catholic, she was going to go to confession prior to Easter Sunday.

The next day, the family car was still parked outside of Sacred Heart Church, but no one knew where Garza was. The question of her location would finally be answered four days after Easter Sunday when her body was found in an irrigation canal near the church. She had not drowned; someone had bludgeoned and suffocated the young woman.

Suspicion was immediately cast on the priest who should have heard her confession the night of her death, 27-year-old Father John Feit. The priest had admitted to listening to the confession in the rectory instead of in the confessional booth where confessions are supposed to occur. One of his fellow priests reported that he had noticed scratches on Feit's hands later than night. Feit also owned the black cord that was found in the canal, which was thought to have been used to bind Garza's hands.

Looking further into Feit's history, the police found that someone of his description had attacked another woman in a nearby church less than a month before Garza died. Feit had been a suspect for that case as well.

The priest was given a polygraph test, and it indicated that he was lying about his role in both cases when he tried to deny the connection to him. Shockingly, Feit would plead no contest yet would not have to serve any time in jail. Nothing was filed against him in the murder of Garza.

It is unknown why nothing was done to the priest, but speculation is that it was due to his prominent role in the Catholic Church. Because of his position, people were either unwilling to question him or felt that nothing would be done because of the role the Catholic Church played in the community.

Opening the Cold Case

Since there was no charge laid against Feit, Garza's case went cold for forty years. It sat in the Texas Rangers' cold cases until 2002, and by this time, Feit had left the priesthood, which meant he no longer had the same protection. There were also more people willing to come forward about what they had seen.

When the case was reopened, another priest came forward to say that Feit had bragged about what he had done when they had lived in a monastery during the 1960s. Although her name may not have been used, Feit had talked about listening to a parishioner's confession, then assaulted her once she finished. He then suffocated her and tossed her into a canal.

The Texas Rangers also sought out the testimony of Father Joseph O'Brien, who had reported the scratches forty years earlier. He insisted on being brought before a grand jury to talk about the information he had on Feit.

The district attorney of Hidalgo County, Rene Guerra, would not accept the evidence, saying that more was needed. Claiming that nothing could be done without either a confession or DNA evidence, Guerra refused to try a case that was several decades old. When people let him know that was unacceptable, he finally took the evidence to a grand jury, but he then refused to let either of the priests with information about Feit to speak. Without those two key pieces of information, the grand jury would not indict the former priest. With the case again unable to progress, it began to go cold.

However, this time, the Texas Rangers would not let it remain dormant, even after the death of Father O'Brien in 2005.

Since the murder, Feit had left the priesthood, married, and had children of his own. He appeared to have lived a quiet life in Arizona, with his crimes being a part of his distant past. This quiet life, however, was not to last.

The Texas Rangers finally got what they needed in terms of support from the district attorney after someone else was elected to the position in 2015. With someone more focused on seeking justice at the helm instead of someone leaving the past in the past, Feit was arrested in early 2016. Now 83, he would have to face his crimes from so long ago in front of a jury, even though that would take a while as he had to be extradited back to Texas, and his legal team also had to come up with his defense. Finally, in November 2017, his trial began. Due to the evidence pointing against him, including the testimony of the priest who had listened to Feit brag about the murder, Feit was convicted a month later. In a symbolic gesture for the number of years that he had evaded justice, the prosecution asked that the 83-year-old be given 57 years in prison. Feit's defense attempted to mitigate his client's actions by pointing to the clean life Feit appeared to have lived since the murder. In the end, though, the jury didn't opt for either option. Instead, they gave Feit a sentence of life in prison (although 57 years would also be a life sentence for someone in his 80s). Thought it had been a long and difficult case because of the politics involved, the Texas Rangers did not give up on finding justice for Irene Garza.

Chapter 17 – Their Role Today

With such an extensive history, the Texas Rangers have undergone many changes to bring them to the point where they are today. Although they are no longer needed for the protection of settlers, they still fight against criminals and work to ensure that criminals are brought to justice no matter how much time has passed since the crime occurred.

Today, the Texas Rangers are one of the divisions of the Texas Department of Public Safety. Their primary role is to lead a number of criminal investigations, which includes:

- Border security
- Major incidents
- Public corruption
- Public integrity
- Shootings involving officers
- Unsolved and serial crimes

From the ten men who once made up the irregular force, there is now more than 200 personnel employed in the division, with 166 of those employees being commissioned as Rangers. The remaining members support the Rangers with a wide range of services, such as:

- Administrative
- Border Security Operations Center

- Joint Operations and Intelligence Centers
- Special Weapons and Tactics

Many of the more specialized services and teams are managed by the Special Operations Group.

The results of their work are tracked fairly closely. The following are the statistics for their work just in 2018:

- 2,726 investigations
- 1,071 felony arrests
- 77 misdemeanor arrests
- 758 confessions
- 524 convictions

Since the turn of the century, their role has continued to shift because of the rise of different threats, particularly terrorism and drug cartel activity. In protecting the citizens from these threats, more specialized departments and teams have been created. While taking on the new threats, the Rangers continue to work on cold cases so that as many people are brought to justice as possible. They also provide a wealth of assistance to regular investigations, providing additional guidance as needed. As one of the states where cartels usually operate, the Texas Rangers have a much better idea of what is happening in that world, as well as how to best protect the people from drug runners and cartel members. They have special permission to enter areas and to work on their own in regions where local officials are either unwilling or unable to keep or restore order. When needed, the Texas Rangers may appear in court at the request of a judge to protect those present, particularly in higher profile cases or in cases where the criminals are dangerous. The agency also has impressive forensic skills, including some of the most current and less common methods, such as hypnosis and facial reconstruction.

They are one of the most recognizable law enforcement agencies in the US, behind the FBI. They do work crimes over state lines as needed to ensure that criminals they have been tracking do not escape.

Conclusion

The Texas Rangers have been around since before Texas gained its independence. Although it was created as a way of protecting settlers, its purpose evolved and changed over nearly two hundred years.

When Texas was a part of Mexico, they were few in number and were composed of volunteers. The combination of many different specialists in the Rangers made them highly effective at protecting settlers from the hostile Native Americans and bandits. They continued to fulfill this role through several wars, acting more as protectors while the citizens fled. Because of the wars, the Rangers were established as a standing force instead of just a group of volunteers. Once Texas became an American state, the role of the Rangers became far less certain. The laws that the people had to follow were no longer something that the Rangers enforced, in part because they did not all know the laws of the US. Texas would also need to resolve state laws that went against the US federal laws, which meant it was uncertain which laws should be upheld and which had to be ignored.

The outbreak of the American Civil War also divided the Rangers. Not all of them believed what the Confederacy stood for, especially after the state had only recently been introduced into the US. Nor did the potential threats from Mexico stop just because the

Civil War was happening. Quite the contrary, it meant that more protection was needed along the borders, as some Mexicans sought to exploit the war to start reclaiming regions for Mexico or to simply raid regions while Texas and the US were more vulnerable. Being divided between different sides and interests would have a very negative effect on the agency, especially as they started to become the agency people turned to for law and order.

The Texas Rangers have not always had a stellar reputation, either. With bigotry being problematic since their inception, there are communities that still have trouble trusting the Rangers today. At one point, the Rangers' behavior was abhorrent because they were unchecked by the government. This allowed them to essentially act like they wrote and enforced the laws.

After being reformed during the 1920s, the Texas Rangers began to take on the current roles they play today, as they evolved into an elite force of lawmen who tended to follow the rules to ensure that they were not committing crimes themselves. Their evolution has helped to make them efficient and effective at capturing some of the most notable criminals in US history.

The Texas Rangers will continue to evolve as laws and politics change. Since they are no longer tied to the whims of the governor or any other single individual, this means that they can ensure that the laws are followed not only by citizens but by people in positions of power.

References

29d. The Mexican-American War, US History, 2019, Independent Hall Association in Philadelphia, www.ushistory.org/

5 Infamous Presidential Assassinations and Attempts, Audrey W., Arcadia Staff, 2020, Arcadia Publishing, www.arcadiapublishing.com/

A Brief History of the Texas Rangers, Mike Cox, 2018, Texas Ranger Hall of Fame and Museum, www.texasranger.org/

African Americans, Bullock Museum, 2020, Bullock Texas State History Museum, www.thestoryoftexas.com/

Agustín de Iturbide – Emperor of Mexico, The Editors of Encyclopedia Britannica, 2020, Encyclopedia Britannica, www.britannica.com/

Austin, Moses, David B. Gracy II, 2020, Texas State Historical Association, tshaonline.org/

Bandit Era in South Texas: Norman Rozeff, May 4, 2014, Summary Planet, www.summaryplanet.com/

Barbed Wire and the Fence Cutting Wars, Ancestry, 2020, www.ancestry.com/

Cherokee War, Handbook of Texas Online, "CHEROKEE WAR," accessed January 05, 2020, Texas State Historical Association, www.tshaonline.org/

Council House Fight, Jodye Lynn Dickson Schilz, 2020, Texas State Historical Association, tshaonline.org/

Father of Texan Independence, Christopher Minister, July 21, 2019, Thought Co., www.thoughtco.com/

Feudin' and Fightin' Friday; Fence Cutting War (Don't Fence Me Out), Sharon Hall, December 20, 2013, Digging History, digging-history.com/

Frank Hammer and the Texas Bandit War of 1915: John Boessenecker, May 6, 2016, The History Readers, www.thehistoryreader.com/

Fredonian Rebellion, Archie P. McDonald, 2020, Texas State Historical Association, tshaonline.org/

Independence and Revolution, 2020, Mexico Newsletter, Mexperience, www.mexperience.com

Joh Wesley Hardin, 1853-1895, Outlaws John Wesley, 2020, FrointerTimes.com, www.frontiertimes.com/

John Wesley Hardin, Famous Texans, 2020, www.famoustexans.com/

Joint Resolution for Annexing Texas to the United States Approved March 1, 1845, Peters, Richard, August 24, 2011, Texas State Library, www.tsl.texas.gov/

Los Diablos Tejanos, Michal Gray, 2000, Images of the West, www.imageswest.digitalimagepro.com/

Martinez, Antonio Maria, Frank Goodwyn, 2020, Texas State Historical Association, tshaonline.org/

Mexican Rule – 1821 – 1835, Katie Whitehurst, 2020, Historical Eras, Texas Our Texas, texasourtexas.texaspbs.org/

Mexican Texas, Arando De Léon, 2020, Texas State Historical Association, tshaonline.org/

Mexican-American War (1846-48), US Navy, August 19, 2019, Naval History and Heritage Command, www.history.navy.mil/

Narrative History of Texas Annexation, Jean Carefoot, August 24, 2011, Texas State Library, www.tsl.texas.gov/

Neches, Battle of the, Hampson Gary, Randolph B. Campbell, 2020, Texas State Historical Association, tshaonline.org/

October 16ᵗʰ, 1909 – Assassin Attacks the President(s), Aloysius Fox, October 16, 2015, Steampunk Symposium, thepandorasociety.com/

Plum Creek, Battle of, Handbook of Texas Online, "PLUM CREEK, BATTLE OF," accessed January 05, 2020, www.tshaonline.org/

Rangers of the Republic of Texas 1836-1845, Texas Ranger Hall of Fame, 2018, www.texasranger.org

Stephen Fuller Austin, PBS, 2001, New Perspectives on The West, www.pbs.org/

Texas Genealogy Trails: Texas Rangers and the Conner Family, Nancy Price, 2020, Genealogy Trails, genealogytrails.com/

Texas Rangers, Ben H. Procter, 2020, Texas State Historical Association, tshaonline.org/

Texas Rangers, Bullock Museum, 2020, Bullock Texas State History Museum, www.thestoryoftexas.com/

Texas Revolution, Jeff Wallenfeldt, 2020, Encyclopedia Britannica Inc, www.britannica.com/

The Bandit War: Old West Tales, October 22, 2018, thoughtsfromafar.blog/

The History of Barbed Wire, Mary Bellis, March 1, 2019, Thought Co, www.thoughtco.com/

The Injustice Never Leaves You, Monica Muñoz Martinez, September 3, 2018, Harvard College, USA

The Mexican American War, PBS, 2020, American Experience, www.pbs.org/

The Mexican-American War in a Nutshell, NCC staff, May 13, 2019, Constitution Daily, National Constitution Center, constitutioncenter.org/

The Secret History of Anti-Mexican Violence in Texas, Carlos Kevin Blanton, September 21, 2018, Texas Monthly, www.texasmonthly.com/

The Story of Sam Bass, Round Rock Texas, 2020, The Historic
Round Rock Collection: An Ongoing
History, www.roundrocktexas.gov/
The Texas Fence-Cutting Wars, Old West Tales, July 29, 2018,
thoughtsfromafar.blog.
The Texas Ranger: Wearing the Cinco Peso, 1821-1900, Mike Cox,
2008, A Tom Doherty Associates Book, NY
The Texas Revolutionary War (1835-1836), 2020, United States
History, www.uswars.net/

Bibliography

"Remember the Alamo!," 1836, EyeWitness to History, 2020, Ibis Communications Inc, www.eyewitnesstohistory.com/

2. Imperial Rivalry II: Spain & France in Tejas (Texas), National Humanities Center, 2020, nationalhumanitiescenter.org/

29d. The Mexican-American War, US History, 2019, Independent Hall Association in Philadelphia, www.ushistory.org/

A Brief History of the Texas Rangers, Mike Cox, 2018, Texas Ranger Hall of Fame and Museum, www.texasranger.org/

Alamo: Monument, San Antonio, Texas, United States, The Editors of Encyclopedia Britannica, 2020, www.britannica.com/

American Indians; A Story Told for Thousands of Years, Bullock Texas State History Museum, 2020, www.thestoryoftexas.com/

Anglo-American Colonization Efforts, Texas State Library, 2020, Archives Commissions, www.tsl.texas.gov/

Anglo-American Colonization, Margaret Swett Henson, 2020, Texas State Historical Association, tshaonline.org/

Apache Indians, Jeffrey D. Carlisle, 2020, Texas State Historical Association, tshaonline.org/

Apollo: Space Program, The Editors of Encyclopedia Britannica, 2020, www.britannica.com/

Causes of Texas Independence, Christopher Minster, May 30, 2019, Thought Co., www.thoughtco.com/

Civil War, Ralph A. Wooster, Brett J. Derbes, 2020, Texas State Historical Association, tshaonline.org/

Conquistadors, Bullock Texas State History Museum, 2020, www.thestoryoftexas.com/

Father of Texan Independence, Christopher Minister, July 21, 2019, Thought Co., www.thoughtco.com/

First Oil Discoveries, America Oil & Gas Historical Society, 2020, aoghs.org/

First Texas Oil Boom, Petroleum Pioneers, 2020, American Oil & Gas Historical Society, aoghs.org/

Fredonian Rebellion, Archie P. McDonald, 2020, Texas State Historical Association, tshaonline.org/

French-Spanish Rivalry in Tejas (Texas), 1685-1690), National Humanities Center, 2020, nationalhumanitiescenter.org/

Gonzales, Battle of, Stephen L. Hardin, 2020, Texas State Historical Association, tshaonline.org/

History of Johnson Space Center, NASA, August 3, 2017, www.nasa.gov/

History of Oil Discoveries in Texas, Texas Almanac, 2020, Texas State Historical Association, texasalmanac.com/

Houston, We've Had a Problem, James A. Lovell, 2020, Apollo Expeditions to the Moon, history.nasa.gov/

Independence and Revolution, 2020, Mexico Newsletter, Mexperience, www.mexperience.com

Joint Resolution for Annexing Texas to the United States Approved March 1, 1845, Peters, Richard, August 24, 2011, Texas State Library, www.tsl.texas.gov/

Los Diablos Tejanos, Michal Gray, 2000, Images of the West, www.imageswest.digitalimagepro.com/

Mexican Rule – 1821 – 1835, Katie Whitehurst, 2020, Historical Eras, Texas Our Texas, texasourtexas.texaspbs.org/

Mexican Rule – 1821 – 1835, Katie Whitehurst, 2020, Historical
Eras, Texas Our Texas, texasourtexas.texaspbs.org/

Mexican Texas, Arando De Léon, 2020, Texas State Historical
Association, tshaonline.org/

Mexican-American War (1846-48), US Navy, August 19, 2019,
Naval History and Heritage Command, www.history.navy.mil/

Narrative History of Texas Annexation, Jean Carefoot, August 24,
2011, Texas State Library, www.tsl.texas.gov/

November 22, 1963: Death of the President, John F. Kennedy
President Library and Museum, 2020, National
Archives, www.jfklibrary.org/

Reconstruction, Carl M. Moneyhon, 2020, Texas State Historical
Association, tshaonline.org/

Remembering the Alamo, Bruce Selcraig, April 1, 2004,
Smithsonian Magazine, www.smithsonianmag.com/

Spanish Colonial 1689-1821, Katie Whitehurst, 2020,
PBS, texasourtexas.texaspbs.org/

Spanish Colonial, Katie Whitehurst, 2020,
PBS, texasourtexas.texaspbs.org/

Stephen Fuller Austin, PBS, 2001, New Perspectives on The
West, www.pbs.org/

Texas During the Civil War, Louis J. Wortham, 2020, Texas
Military Forces Museum, www.texasmilitaryforcesmuseum.org/

Texas Rangers, Bullock Museum, 2020, Bullock Texas State History
Museum, www.thestoryoftexas.com/

Texas Revolution, Jeff Wallenfeldt, 2020, Encyclopedia Britannica
Inc, www.britannica.com/

Texas: State, United States, Gregory Lewis McNamee, DeWitt C.
Reddick, Ralph A. Wooster, January 17, 2020, Encyclopedia
Britannica, www.britannica.com/

The Apollo Mission, NASA, February 1, 2019, www.nasa.gov/

The Comanche – Horsemen of the Plains, Legends of America,
2020, www.legendsofamerica.com/

The Mexican American War, PBS, 2020, American
Experience, www.pbs.org/

The Mexican-American War in a Nutshell, NCC staff, May 13,
2019, Constitution Daily, National Constitution
Center, constitutioncenter.org/

The Republic for Texas – The Texas Revolution Texas Declaration
of Independence, Texas State Library, 2020, www.tsl.texas.gov/

The Spanish Colonial Era in Texas, study.com, 2020, study.com/

The Start of the Space Race, Khan Academy,
2020, www.khanacademy.org/

The Texas Revolutionary War (1835-1836), 2020, United States
History, www.uswars.net/

Three Shots Fired at President Kennedy's Motorcade..., Texas State
Library, 2020, www.tsl.texas.gov/

Why the Public Stopped Believing the Government about JFK's
Murder, Steve M. Gillon, November 21, 2019, History, A&E
Television Networks, www.history.com/

Here's another book by Captivating History
that you might be interested

i

Made in United States
North Haven, CT
09 May 2022

19048482R00139